May courage and strength

guide your heart always!

Rochelle Jennings Coe

Believe in Yourself

Believe in Yourself

Live a Life of Courage, Determination, & Strength of Heart

RochellePennington

Published by Pathways Press
1-800-503-5507

ISBN: 978-0-9740810-5-2

Published by Pathways Press 1-800-503-5507

Rochelle Pennington wishes to thank her husband, Leslie, for all of his love and support over the past thirty years. "*He is at the heart of all I accomplish.*"

Rochelle Pennington may be scheduled for speaking engagements by calling: 1-800-503-5507

Manufactured in Canada

Dedicated to John Smith

You are loved.

Table of Contents

Choose an Attitude of Altitude

"A positive attitude makes it easier to get up in the morning—and also to move up in the world."

ZIG ZIGLAR

1. Always remember that your thoughts are energy, and you can make or break your world by your thinking.

SUSAN TAYLOR

Nothing on earth can stop the man with the right mental attitude from achieving his goal, and nothing on earth can help the man with the wrong mental attitude.

THOMAS JEFFERSON

2. Concentrate on the positive.

WILL GARCIA

I'm in a wonderful position: I'm unknown, I'm underrated, and there's nowhere to go but up.

PIERRE S. DUPONT IV

It's a Matter of Attitude

The true story is told of two American salesmen who were employed by a large shoe company. Each was sent on an assignment to the continent of Africa.

Within twenty-four hours of the first salesman's arrival, he wired a message back to the main office which read, "RETURNING HOME IMMEDIATELY. HOPELESS SITUATION. NO ONE HERE WEARS SHOES."

Communication from the second salesman followed shortly thereafter: "CAN'T WAIT TO GET STARTED! UNLIMITED POTENTIAL! NO ONE HERE HAS ANY SHOES!"

Attitude is powerful. It is also a choice.

As is our confidence, so is our capacity.

WILLIAM HAZLITT

3. Remember that it's not who we are that holds us back; it's who we think we're not.

MICHAEL NOLAN

If we could get cellulite put onto Barbie dolls, it would help a lot of people with their self-acceptance.

SARK

4. Understand that the only limit to your realization of tomorrow will be your doubts of today.

FRANKLIN ROOSEVELT

We can do only what we think we can do. We can be only what we think we can be. We can have only what we think we can have. What we do, what we are, what we have, all depend upon what we think.

ROBERT COLLIER

5. Form the habit of making decisions when your spirit is fresh. To let dark moods lead you is like choosing cowards to command your armies.

CHARLES COOLEY

There will always be times when you feel discouraged. I, too, have felt despair many times in my life, but I do not keep a chair for it. I will not entertain it. It is not allowed to eat from my plate.

CLARISSA PINKOLA ESTES

6. Give consideration to the fact that you will block your dream if you allow your fear to grow bigger than your faith.

MARY MANIN MORRISSEY

A person who doubts himself is like a man who would enlist in the ranks of his enemies and bear arms against himself. He makes his failure certain because he himself is the first person to be convinced of it.

ALEXANDER DUMAS

The Magic Sword

There is an old, old story from the days of knights in shining armor, about a very ordinary youth who was afraid to test his skill at arms on the tournament field. Some of his friends, thinking to have some fun with him, presented him with a sword which they said possessed an ancient, magical power, and the man who wielded it could never meet defeat in battle.

To their amazement, the youth sprang to the field and quickly put the gift to use, winning game after game.

Never had anyone witnessed such speed and daring at arms.

With each tournament, the news of his artistry spread, and before long he was hailed as the foremost knight of the realm.

At last, thinking it would now do no harm, one of his friends revealed the joke and confided that the instrument contained no magic at all, but was just an ordinary sword.

Terror seized the young knight's heart. His legs shook beneath him on the field of combat. His breath caught in his throat, and his fingers lost all grip. No longer able to believe in his sword, he, sadly, could not believe in himself and never fought again.

THE MORAL COMPASS

7. Whatever you can dream, begin it; boldness has genius, power, and magic in it.

GOETHE

Act as if it were impossible to fail.

DOROTHEA BRANDE

8. Forge forward. You will gain strength, courage, and confidence by every experience in which you really stop to look fear in the face. You must do the thing you think you cannot do.

ELEANOR ROOSEVELT

I have gone ahead despite the pounding in my heart that says, "Turn back!"

ERICA JONG

I am an optimist. It does not seem too much use being anything else.

WINSTON CHURCHILL

Believe It, Achieve It

It's time to think about what you're thinking about.

JOEL OLSTEEN

In the *Star Wars* movie, *The Empire Strikes Back*, Luke Skywalker flies his spaceship to a swamp planet on a personal quest. There he seeks out a Jedi master named Yoda to teach him the ways of becoming a Jedi warrior. Luke wants to free the galaxy from the oppression of the evil tyrant Darth Vader.

Yoda agrees to help Luke and begins by teaching him how to lift rocks with his mental powers.

Then, one day, Yoda tells Luke to lift his ship out from the swamp where it sank after a crash landing. Luke complains that lifting rocks is one thing, but lifting a star-fighter spaceship is quite another matter. Yoda insists. Luke manages a valiant effort but fails in his attempt.

Yoda then focuses his mind, and lifts the ship with ease. Luke, dismayed, exclaims, "I don't believe it!"

"That's why you couldn't lift it," Yoda replied. "You didn't believe you could."

MARK LINK

9. Proceed with confidence, as though the limit of your ability does not exist.

PIERRE TEILHARD DE CHARDIN

I've gone through my life believing in the strength and competence of others, but never in my own. Now, dazzled, I have discovered that my capacities are real. It was like I had found a fortune in the lining of an old coat.

JOAN MILLS

10. Tap your potential.

SHEILA MURRAY BETHEL

All you need is deep within you waiting to unfold and reveal itself. All you have to do is be still and take time to seek for what is within, and you will surely find it.

EILEEN CADDY

Believing is Seeing

Ask and it will be given to you; seek and you will find; knock and the door will be opened to you.

MATTHEW 7:7

Nothing will be impossible for you.

MATTHEW 17:20-21

What you decide on will be done.

JOB 22:28

Believe that you have received it and it will be yours.

MARK 11:24-25

According to your faith it will be done to you.

MATTHEW 9:29

By His power He may fulfill every good purpose of yours and every act prompted by your faith.

II THESSALONIANS 1:11

Have faith and do not doubt.

MATTHEW 21:21

Then Peter got down out of the boat, walked on the water, and came toward Jesus. But when Peter saw the wind, he was afraid and, beginning to sink, cried out, “Lord, save me!” Immediately Jesus reached out his hand and caught him. “You of little faith,” he said to Peter, “Why did you doubt?”

MATTHEW 14:29-31

Don’t be afraid; just believe.

LUKE 8:50

Ask and you will receive.

JOHN 16:24

Everything is possible to him who believes.

MARK 9:23

When he asks, he must believe and not doubt, because he who doubts is like a wave of the sea, blown and tossed by the wind. That man should not think he will receive anything…he is doubleminded and unstable.

JAMES 1:6-7

I tell you the truth, if anyone says to this mountain, “Go, throw yourself into the sea,” and does not doubt in his heart but believes that what he says will happen, it will be done for him.

MARK 11:23

Faith is being sure of what we hope for and certain of what we do not see.

HEBREWS 11:1

11. Never forget that whether you think you can, or you think you can't, you're right.

HENRY FORD

It will be done just as you believed it would.

MATTHEW 8:10

12. Do not impose limitations upon your beliefs or you will limit the creative capacity of your consciousness.

ALAN VAUGHAN

The mind is more vulnerable than the stomach because it can be poisoned without feeling immediate pain.

HELEN MacINNES

Negative attitudes are educated into us, and can, if we wish, be educated out.

DR. KARL MENNINGER

What Can a Quarter Buy You?

It's amazing what a little courage in the right place at the right time can accomplish.

JOHN SCHERER

I do believe it was the best twenty-five cents I ever spent. It went into a parking meter on the corner of Sheboygan Street and Marr Street, one block off of the downtown area in Fond du Lac, Wisconsin. My quarter bought me exactly one hour of time.

I had parked in this spot many times before because it gave me easy access to the public library. On the particular morning I am referring to, however, instead of turning left, crossing the street, and entering the library, I headed to the right where the Windhover Center for the Arts was located. A friend telephoned me the day prior to let me know about a traveling VSA (Very Special Arts) exhibit on display there. "You really must see this," she told me of the collection of artwork done by disabled children.

Beneath a bright blue sky on a very February morn, I headed toward the magnificent, older building, restored to its original grandeur not long ago.

I entered and ascended several polished, wooden stairs. Atop them, a burgundy and ivory oriental rug was laid, and I paused on it to sign the visitor guest book.

From where I stood, the children's artwork was visible already, hung from just beyond the double doorway entrance into the lovely gallery. The first painting—colorful, vibrant, and seemingly alive—faced me. It was titled *The Dancing Flowers*. I smiled as I read the words, and would do so again and again during the time I spent among the children. They were not there physically, and yet they were there, having painted a piece of themselves onto their canvases in watercolors, oils, and pastels. You could sense their presence, and you could sense who they were—and what they loved—in paintings they titled *It's Great Being Me, My Playroom, Swimming Along, I Enjoy It,* and *The Magnificent Sunflower*.

Beside each piece, a framed biography was hung which listed the name, age, and disability of each child. These little artists suffered from many impairments—Cerebral Palsy, Down Syndrome, Autism, Spinal Muscular Strophy, seizures, and other varied physical and emotional disabilities. Some lived in wheelchairs, like 10-year-old Brittany. There were no easy paths. This was clear.

Yet despite challenges so enormous I could not even begin to imagine what these youngsters faced daily, each had expressed himself or herself from a place of beauty within.

Like Sarah. Although crippled from a disease which prevented her from even grasping onto a paintbrush, she still brought forth her masterpiece, *Harvest*. How did she do this? By having a paintbrush attached to her forehead. I stopped for a moment and considered Sarah, amazing Sarah. Her courage left an impression on me that I have not forgotten.

Courage is a way of life for these youngsters. And so is hope. You see it in their art, and you hear it in their words hanging beside their paintings. Eleven-year-old Julia told in her bio that one day she would fulfill her dream of becoming a famous woman artist. Twelve-year-old John Magnusson believed we can all experience the hopes our hearts harbor. He wrote, "You can do anything you put your mind to."

Anything. All of us. Thank you, John, for being our reminder that our dreams can take flight like the hummingbirds and butterflies and bumblebees that filled the room, painted by those disabled in body, but not in soul, painted by those "focusing on their ability and not on their dis," as one little girl so wonderfully put it.

I left the art gallery a different person than the one I had been when I arrived. I knew this as I sat in a little coffee shop around the corner afterward, sipping tea, lemon ginger with just a bit of honey. I thought about starfish swimming in the ocean as I sat there quietly and watched the world go by. Ten-year-old Diane Jacobson had painted several. Miss Diane believed that starfish enjoy, most of all, being together, another wonderful word.

Together, we open one another's eyes to truths we know, but have sometimes forgotten. Together, we help those unable to help themselves in some ways, and they, in turn, will help us in others. Someone, somewhere has helped these children, and I find myself profoundly grateful to each of these persons who I know not the name of, nor they mine.

We place a paintbrush in these young hands, and it is grasped. Then something within is awakened. Or we attach such a paintbrush to a forehead and for doing so, we will be taken to places where we can see the world through beautiful, beautiful eyes.

I finished my tea that day, and placed the sage green and orchid-colored ceramic mug I drank it from back on the table. For a while, I simply sat and admired the magnificent piece of pottery, hand-thrown and crafted by a local artist with an extraordinary talent and an ordinary name: John Smith. His work is incredibly interesting for many reasons, not the least of which is that Mr. Smith is blind.

ROCHELLE PENNINGTON

Almost everybody walks around with a vast burden of imaginary limitations inside his head. While the burden remains, success is as difficult to achieve as the conquest of Mount Everest with a sack of rocks tied to your back.

J. H. BRENNAN

Did you know?

Explorer Robert Peary failed seven times in his attempt to reach the North Pole. He finally succeeded in 1909 after exclaiming, "I must have it!" His gravestone is etched with the words of his personal credo: Inveniam Viam Aut Facium, *"I shall find a way or make one!"*

13. Remember that you will lose much by fearing to attempt.

J. N. MOFFIT

Sometimes you just have to take the leap and build your wings on the way down.

KOBI YAMADA

14. Understand that every situation has two handles. You can grab it by the handle of fear or by the handle of faith.

HENRY WARD BEECHER

The first thing I had to conquer was fear. I realized what a debilitating thing fear is. It can render you absolutely helpless.

BRYAN JANIS

I have learned this at least by my experiments: If one advances confidently in the direction of his dreams, and endeavors to live the life which he has imagined, he will meet with success unexpected in common hours.

HENRY DAVID THOREAU

15. Realize that your mind can focus on fear, worry, negativity, or despair. Or it can focus on confidence, opportunity, solutions, optimism, and success. You decide.

DON WARD

The biggest quality in successful people is an impatience with negative thinking.

EDWARD McCABE

16. Don't doubt, or you'll be out.

JERRY FREKING

The pessimist is half-licked before he starts.

THOMAS BUCKNER

17. Effectiveness and happiness depend upon the kinds of thoughts you think. It is absolutely impossible to be effective and happy if you continue to think unhappiness-producing thoughts. If you put into your mind thoughts of fear, you will get thoughts of fear out of your mind. Fill your mind with failure attitudes, and failure will emerge. Whatever the condition of your mind, begin now to displace unhealthy thoughts—driving them from your mind—and replace them with positive thoughts.

NORMAN VINCENT PEALE

No philosophy will help a man to succeed when he is always doubting his ability to do so. No matter how hard you work for success, if your thoughts are saturated with the fear of failure, they will kill your efforts, neutralize your endeavors, and make success impossible.

CHARLES BAUDOUIN

As You Think

There exists the Law of the Fallow Field. Simply stated, this law holds that if nothing positive is planted in the garden, it will always revert to weeds. So, we have to continually plant each growing season exactly what it is we expect to grow. If nothing of value is planted, nothing of value will be harvested.

BRIAN CAVANAUGH

Your mind may be likened to a garden that may be intelligently cultivated or allowed to run wild; but whether cultivated or neglected, it must—and will—bring forth. If no useful seeds are put into it, then an abundance of useless weed seeds will fall therein, and will continue to produce their kind.

Just as gardeners cultivate their plots, keeping them free from weeds, and growing the flowers and fruits they desire, so may you tend the garden of your mind, weeding out all the wrong, useless, and impure thoughts, and cultivating toward perfection the flowers and fruits of right, useful, and pure thoughts. By pursuing this process, you will sooner or later discover that you are the master gardener of your soul, the director of your life. You also reveal, within yourself, the laws of thought, and understand, with ever-increasing accuracy, how the forces of thought—and the elements of the mind—operate in the shaping of your character, circumstances, and destiny.

You are where you are by the law of your being. The thoughts that you have built into your character have brought you there, and in the arrangement of your life there is no element of chance, but all is the result of a law that cannot err.

And so we are held prisoners only by ourselves. Our own thoughts and actions are the jailers of our fate—they imprison if they are base; they are also the angels of freedom—they liberate if they are noble.

Most of us are anxious to improve our circumstances, but are unwilling to improve ourselves—and we therefore remain bound. If we do not shrink from honest self-examination, we can never fail to accomplish the object our hearts are set upon.

Good thoughts and actions do not produce bad results; bad thoughts and actions do not produce good results. We understand this law in the natural world, and work with it; but few understand it in the mental and moral world—although its operation there is just as simple and undeviating.

To live continually in thoughts of ill will, cynicism, self-pity, suspicion, and envy, is to be confined in a self-made prison cell. But to think well of all, to be cheerful with all, to patiently learn to find the good in all—such unselfish thoughts are the very portals of heaven.

JAMES ALLEN

He who would be happy, strong, and useful must cease to be a passive receptacle for the negative, beggarly, and impure streams of thought, and as a wise householder commands his servants and invites his guests, so must he learn to command his thinking, and to say, with authority, what thoughts he shall allow into the mansion of his soul.

ANONYMOUS

18. Don't cultivate fear, or it will grow stronger. Cultivate faith, and it will achieve the mastery. Faith is the stronger emotion because it is positive, whereas fear is negative.

JOHN PAUL JONES

We can change ourselves for the better, and cause ourselves to subconsciously pursue our most precious desires with almost total success, if we crystallize the images clearly enough in our minds because the subconscious mind cannot tell the difference between real and vividly imagined situations.

CHARLES A. COONRADT

19. Dream lofty dreams, and as you dream, so shall you become. Your vision is the promise of what you shall at last unveil.

JOHN RUSKIN

Only you can deprive yourself of anything. Do not oppose this realization, for it is truly the beginning of the dawn of light.

A COURSE IN MIRACLES

20. Don't allow yourself to continually focus on how difficult your goal is or you will never achieve it.

CYNTHIA KERSEY

A positive attitude is a magnet for positive results.

ANONYMOUS

21. Understand that your attitude at the beginning of a difficult undertaking will, more than anything else, determine its outcome.

WILLIAM JAMES

The world has a way of giving what is demanded of it. If you are frightened and look for failure, you will get it, no matter how hard you may try to succeed. Lack of faith in yourself, in what life will do for you, cuts you off from the good things of the world. Expect victory and you make victory. Nothing is truer than this.

PRESTON BRADLEY

22. Look for the opportunity in every difficulty, instead of being paralyzed at the thought of difficulty in every opportunity.

WALTER COLE

When Goliath came against the Israelites, the soldiers all thought, "He's so big we can never kill him." David looked at the same giant and thought, "He's so big I can't miss."

RUSS JOHNSON

23. To bring anything into your life, imagine that it is already there.

ANONYMOUS

There is a law in psychology that says if you form a picture in your mind of what you would like to be, and keep that picture there long enough, you will soon become exactly as you have been thinking.

WILLIAM JAMES

The Golden Formula

What are your hopes? What are your dreams? Do you believe that you can reach them?

Step number one in reaching a goal is determining what your goal is. Step number two is maintaining a positive expectation of meeting it.

When positive expectation is released regarding the outcome of a situation, this positive energy pulls other positive energy into our life, helping us along our way. The same is true of doubt. When doubt and fear are released, they, too, connect with energy, but it is a negative energy that is pulled in, an energy that will work directly against us. Thus, a person's own doubt becomes his or her greatest obstacle, blocking access to positive energy and positive results, and a person's own fear becomes the most significant hindrance to experiencing the best life has to offer each of us. Doubt creates more doubt, and fear does the same.

In the pages of this book, examples are given to illustrate "really happened" successes that began with hope. Seemingly impossible dreams started coming true for persons up against staggering odds—a blind man who want to ski, an amputee who want to climb mountains, and for a young man who was told he would never walk again but set his heart on becoming a world-class runner. How did these incredible, incredible dreams come true? Simple: Their possessors didn't expect them not to.

Although these stories detail different accomplishments, there is one common denominator. It is this: Each person held fast to an unshakable confidence—and an unwaveringly hope—in their ability to reach their desired destination. And hope is powerful. It, too, multiplies upon itself, creating more hope, and more and more.

"We begin to receive when we begin to believe." This single sentence, handed down through the ages, conveys a profound spiritual truth: Our beliefs release a spiritual power in our lives. We call forth into physical existence that which first exists within our minds. This is both the good news and the bad news because faith operates in two dimensions—positive and negative. Positive faith is evidenced by hope, and negative faith is evidenced by fear.

Which of these is the driving force of your life? Does positive energy dominate your life or negative energy? Do you generally believe more often that things will turn out for the best, or do you expect them to turn out for the worst? Spend some time today thinking about your answers to these questions and reminding yourself that what you believe you will receive. These simple reflections can significantly raise your awareness as to how much of your thinking is rooted in doubt.

Several years ago I completed a Bible study on the subject of fear. It was fascinating to me to discover that there are 365 specific warnings about the power of negative faith found in the attitudes of fear and doubt. The scriptures warn us to "fear not, worry not, be not afraid, be not terrified, have faith, and do not doubt." A reminder is provided for every single day of the year. I wondered why.

I believe the answer to that very question can be found in the Biblical book of James 1:6-8 where we are told we must "believe and not doubt because he who doubts is like a wave of the sea, blown and tossed by the wind. That man should not think he will receive anything…he is a double–minded man, unstable in all he does."

In all honesty, these verses bothered me for a good long time. I simply could not understand why heaven would withhold goodness from a person simply because he or she was fearful or doubtful. But then it clicked: Heaven doesn't withhold anything from us. *We* withhold.

When we are hoping for something positive, we are sending out a positive energy. This energy has the power to create what we believe. But then, if we begin to doubt what we hope for, we are sending out a negative energy which also has the power to create what we believe. Our doubt then negates—*cancels out*—our positive energy. We receive "nothing" because the energy is returned to zero. A positive combined with a negative will mathematically yield an end result of zero.

The analogy of a wave, blown and tossed, is quite fitting. How often do we find ourselves believing something good will happen, but then end up convincing ourselves it probably won't? "Yes it will, no it won't; yes it will, no it won't." We toss back and forth in double mindedness and accomplish little or nothing.

Fear. Its grip is powerful, leaving us helpless and defeated when we submit to it.

How does a person begin the process of replacing fear with faith? How does positive faith operate?

Positive faith is released "through love." And so, as we stand in positive faith in regards to our hopes and dreams, we must also stand in positive attitudes in our commitment to love others. Our life is one big picture. Everything is connected. Everything matters. And there is an undeniable connection between living a loving life and living an accomplished life.

As an example, we find in Mark's Gospel one of many direct links between powerful living and our relationships with others. In chapter 11, verses 22-25, we read: "Have faith in God…I tell you the truth, if anyone says to this mountain, 'Go, throw yourself into the sea,' and does not doubt in his heart but believes that what he says will happen, it will be done for him. Therefore I tell you, whatever you ask for in prayer, believe that you have received it, and it will be yours. And when you stand praying, if you hold anything against anyone, forgive."

Two seemingly unrelated subjects are lined up side-by-side in this teaching—belief and forgiveness. The message of these words is clear. Fear will block our paths—every aspect of fear, including unforgiveness. The negative attitudes of fear can be manifested in many forms—resentment, anger, gossip, hate, doubt. These are all spiritual roadblocks that will work directly against the power of positive faith which operates through love. Our attitudes toward life, and our attitudes toward others, are directly linked to our goals.

Goals. What are yours? Are you ready to begin to believe and achieve?

Before any of us can move forward, we must first be willing to take responsibility for our life up until this point. Then, we must make the determination to continue to do so from this point on. This means owning up to the fact that we have had something to do with where we find ourselves in life right now. It is a process that takes honesty, and it also takes courage.

It may take more time to do this than one would at first suppose—especially if we have been in the habit of blaming others for our life—or in the habit of making excuses.

However, no matter how difficult it is to get serious about this important first step, it is a step which must be taken. It is only when we understand that our choices—our own choices—are at the root of our blessing, will we be able to move forward in life in a more positive and productive way.

Our lives are made up of, and defined by, moments. Just moments. Think connect-the-dots. Each experience of our life, in and of itself, may seem insignificant, but when added to another experience, and still more others, a picture slowly begins to emerge of who we are and what we have become.

The "big picture" of our life didn't just show up on the scene one day. It emerged. Little by little, choice by choice, we were defining our days and defining our lives. Thus, all those little things were really the big thing.

Once you've taken responsibility for the choices you have made in your life, next determine what your goals are from here. Get clear on what it is you want. Narrow it down. What is it *exactly*?

After you begin to focus on your specific plans, get a mental picture of them within your mind. Visualize your expectations. "See" yourself succeeding. When a positive image is sent forth from your mind, an important step is taken toward the materialization of your vision into reality.

Next, remind yourself: "If I don't believe, I won't receive." Understanding this concept is key. It is absolutely, positively key. As important as it is to get decisive about what your goals are, it is equally important to believe that you can reach them.

If self-doubt persists, re-read the true stories given as examples in order to reinforce your understanding of the fact that nothing is impossible. Consider each story and reflect on the extreme challenges that were overcome by sheer human determination stretched to remarkable limits, stories about individuals who easily could have allowed the circumstances of their lives to convince them that all was hopeless. Instead, they decided that their lives would not be defined by their circumstances. They determined that they would be bigger than their circumstances and bigger than their obstacles. Each remained open to believing that life still offered infinite possibilities. Rather than focusing on the "why" question of their handicap or their past, they focused on the "where" they intended to go from that point on and "how" they intended to get there. "Where," "how," and "when" are positive questions we can ask ourselves because these questions will call us into action and responsibility.

Know this: It matters not nearly as much where you have been, as it matters where you are committed to go from here. Regardless if your life before this moment has been filled with regrets, what matters most is not what you have done in the past, or where you have been, but what you now intend to do with where you have been and with what you have done.

Right now, at this moment, your life can begin changing for the better—and for the best. Each of us has equal access to the positive mental mindsets and loving attitudes that are the driving force behind successful living. When we commit to livingly lovingly, and when we commit to replacing our self-doubts, our self-condemnations, our fears, and our excuses—"I'm too young, too old, too poor, too inexperienced"—with positive actions and positive beliefs, great things happen.

Through consistent, small steps made daily, we begin to discover these small steps are yielding big differences in our lives.

Every effort we put forth toward achieving our goals multiplies unto itself until we find we are living our best life—a life that has evolved from our dream into our reality.

ROCHELLE PENNINGTON

24. Live large. Whatever you can conceive and believe you can achieve.

NAPOLEON HILL

Did I not tell you that if you believed, you would see?

JOHN 11:40

25. Before going to bed each night, think for five minutes about the achievement possibilities of the morrow. This will steadily and increasingly bear fruit in your life, particularly if all ideas of difficulty, worry, and fear are resolutely ruled out and replaced by visions of accomplishment and smiling courage.

ANONYMOUS

The greatest discovery of any generation is that humans can alter their lives by altering the attitudes of their minds.

WILLIAM JAMES

26. Realize that everything is in the mind. That's where it all starts. And knowing what you want is the first step toward getting it.

MAE WEST

Man decides what his existence will be, what he will become in the next moment.

VIKTOR FRANKL

27. Never forget that there is very little difference in people, but that little difference makes a big difference. The little difference is attitude. The big difference is whether it is positive or negative.

CLEMENT STONE

If I were to wish for anything, I should not wish for wealth and power, but for the passionate sense of the potential, for the eye which, ever young and ardent, sees the possible.

SOREN KIERKEGAARD

Surmounting Life's Peaks

Your thoughts have the power to determine your conduct for the day. Optimistic thoughts will make your day bright and productive, while pessimistic thinking will make it wasteful. Face each day cheerfully, smilingly, and bravely.

WILLIAM M. PECK

The next time you are faced with a seemingly insurmountable task, consider the hurdles Erik Weihermayer has overcome.

Erik has worked as a middle-school teacher, run marathons, and performed acrobatic skydiving stunts. He's also a scuba diver, downhill skier, and long-distance bicyclist. Those are impressive accomplishments for any 32-year-old. However, Erik has been blind since age thirteen when a degenerative eye disease destroyed his retinas.

But being blind has not prevented him from embracing all that life has to offer. Recently, Erik hit a new personal high by becoming the first blind climber to reach the top of Mount Everest, the tallest challenge in the world for any mountaineer.

"I just kept telling myself to be focused," Erik explained to a CNN interviewer after his ascent. "Be full of energy. Keep relaxed. Don't let all those distractions—the fear and the doubt—creep into your brain because they will ruin you."

That's good advice for climbing any kind of mountain—be it made of rock or something more personal

BITS AND PIECES

28. Remember that you are not entitled to happiness; you are only entitled to "the pursuit" of it. You have to catch up with it yourself.

BENJAMIN FRANKLIN

If you observe a really happy man, you will find him building a boat, writing a symphony, educating his son, growing double dahlias in his garden, and looking for dinosaur eggs in the Gobi Desert. He will not be searching for happiness as if it were a collar button that rolled under the radiator. He will not be striving for it as a goal in itself. He will have become aware that he is happy living the course of life as positively and as fully as possible each day.

W. BERAN WOLF

Believe in the Greatness Within You

"I saw an angel in the marble and I carved until I set him free."

MICHAELANGELO, sculptor of
"The Prisoner"

29. Whatever you do, you are going to need courage. Whatever course you decide upon, there will always be someone to tell you that you are wrong. Difficulties will arise which will tempt you to believe that your critics are right, but you must map out your course of action and follow it to the end.

RALPH WALDO EMERSON

If you worry about what people think of you, it's because you have more confidence in their opinion than you do in your own.

ANONYMOUS

30. Always remember that nothing splendid was ever achieved except by those who dared believe that something inside them was superior to circumstances.

BRUCE BARTON

It had long since come to my attention that people of accomplishment rarely sat back and let things happen to them. They went out and happened to things.

ELINOR SMITH

A Creative Solution

According to legend, when Michelangelo started out, he was ignored by his own generation and disdained by the art critics. But he had faith in his ability, and he decided to use subterfuge on his critics.

He knew that they were fascinated when someone excavated a site of old ruins and dug up a supposedly priceless work of art. So Michelangelo decided to stain one of his sculptures to make it look ancient. He then buried it where he was certain that an excavating party was sure to find it, near the ruins.

When the sculpture was uncovered and lifted from the earth, the art critics were enraptured. They pronounced it a work of exceptional beauty and rare value. The Cardinal of San Giorgio was so impressed with it that he paid a large sum of money to acquire the piece for his collection.

It was at this point that Michelangelo came forward and confessed his hoax. The art critics were stunned. They had no choice but to finally admit that he was an artistic genius.

From then on, Michaelangelo was commissioned to do important works and became one of the most renown artists in history.

BRIAN CAVANAUGH

31. Keep away from people who try to belittle your ambitions. Small people always do that, but the really great make you feel that you, too, can become great.

MARK TWAIN

My mother said to me, "If you become a soldier, you'll be a general; if you become a monk, you'll end up as the pope." Instead, I became a painter and wound up as Picasso.

PABLO PICASSO

32. Believe in yourself even if no one else will.

SUGAR RAY ROBINSON

Permit no one to dissuade you from pursuing the goals you set for yourself.

RALPH BUNCHE

Do not be afraid to use what talents you possess for how silent the woods would be if no birds sang except those which sang best.

HENRY VAN DYKE

The Power of Perseverance

A young man in Kansas City, with a burning desire to draw, went from newspaper to newspaper trying to sell his cartoons. Each editor he contacted coldly and quickly suggested that he had no talent—and "lacked creativity"—and implied that the young man might want to choose another line of work.

But the young man persevered, determined to make his dream a reality. He wanted to draw, and draw he would.

For several months, he kept knocking on doors, and the rejections kept coming. Finally, a church hired him to draw publicity material.

Working out of an old, mouse-infested garage, the young man befriended one of the little creatures. Ironically, in this less-than-ideal working environment, his most famous work was stimulated. He called the mouse "Mickey."

Walt Disney was on his way.

SEEDS FROM THE SOWER

33. Don't listen to people who come up with reasons why you can't do what you want to do—including yourself.

H. JACKSON BROWN

Nobody's going to rain on my parade, especially me.

HALLIE BROOKS

34. Understand that the only way to avoid criticism is to do nothing, say nothing, and be nothing.

ELBERT HUBBARD

It took me a long time not to judge myself through someone else's eyes. I never really address myself anymore to any image anybody has of me. That's like fighting with ghosts.

SALLY FIELDS

When we line up all the facts we think are against us, the facts can stop us before we start. Whatever we need to discourage us—I'm too young, too old, too short, too tall, unprepared, inexperienced, or not quite ready—we can uncover. And if we miss a few, we can always find someone to help us "face the facts." The facts, after all, speak for themselves—except they're not true.

MARLO THOMAS

35. Give consideration to the fact that great men and women are frequently misjudged by others before they become famous.

ALAN McGINNIS

"Albert is a very poor student. He is mentally slow (and possibly retarded), unsocialable, and forever adrift in his silly dreams. He is spoiling it for the rest of the class. It would be in the best interests of all if he were removed from school at once."

COMMENTS ABOUT ALBERT EINSTEIN
Einstein did not speak until he was four years old and only learned to read much later than other students. Einstein's parents were told by another teacher that it didn't matter what profession the boy prepared for because he would never be successful at anything. Einstein left school at the age of fifteen so "he wouldn't set a bad example for the rest of the students." He went on to become the greatest scientist of the twentieth century.

"Woodrow is a unique member of the class. He is ten years old and is only just beginning to read and write. He shows signs of improving, but you must not set your sights too high for him."

COMMENTS ABOUT WOODROW WILSON

"Abraham is a daydreamer and asks foolish questions."

COMMENTS ABOUT ABRAHAM LINCOLN

If You Can Dream It, You Can Do It

Many of us are afraid to follow our passions, to pursue what we want most because it means taking risks, facing rejection, and even failing. But to pursue your passion with all of your heart and soul is success in itself. The greatest failure is to have never even tried.

ROBYN ALLAN

1927: Lucille Ball entered the John Murray Anderson Drama School in hopes of becoming an actress but was told by the head instructor: "Try any other profession. Any other."

Lucille Ball went on to become one of the most recognized actresses of the twentieth century, and even stared in her own sitcom, the *I Love Lucy* show.

1933: Fred Astaire auditioned at MGM Studios. The director critiqued him as follows: "Can't act. Slightly bald. Can dance a little."

Astaire went on to become one of the world's most accomplished dancers. He hung the "can dance a little" memo from years earlier over the fireplace in his Beverly Hills home.

1944: Marilyn Monroe contacted the Blue Book Modeling Agency with her dream of becoming a model. The director there, Emmeline Snively, told Monroe that she didn't have a chance in the industry and encouraged her to "learn secretarial work or else get married."

Marilyn Monroe went on to become one of the most recognized faces in the world.

1954: Elvis Presley quit his truck driving job because he had a dream of becoming a singer. He was fired at the Grand Ole Opry after only one performance. The manager there, Jimmy Denny, told Presley: "You ain't goin' nowhere, son. You ought to go back to drivin' a truck."

Presley went on to become "The King of Rock and Roll."

1956: Buddy Holly was fired from the Decca Recording Company. He was told by the manager, Paul Cohen, that he was "the biggest no-talent I ever worked with."

Buddy Holly continued to pursue his dream and became a household name. *Rolling Stones* magazine later named Holly one of "the major influences on the rock music of the sixties."

1959: Two unknown, hopeful actors, Burt Reynolds and Clint Eastwood, ironically showed up at the same Universal Studios audition. Both were rejected. Burt Reynolds was told: "You have no talent. None." Clint Eastwood was told: "You have a chip on your tooth, your Adam's apple sticks out too far, and you talk too slow."

Despite heartbreaking rejections early in their careers, both men persevered and went on to become mega-stars in the movie industry.

1962: Four young musicians auditioned for the Decca Recording Company. The executives there were unimpressed with the British rock group that called themselves The Beatles, and they turned them down with these words: "We don't like your sound. Groups of guitars are on their way out."

If I were asked to give what I consider to be the single most useful bit of advice for all humanity, it would be this: Expect trouble as an inevitable part of life and when it comes, hold your head high, look it squarely in the eye, and say, “I will be bigger than you. You cannot defeat me.”

ANN LANDERS

Against All Odds

One day a partially deaf boy came home from school with a note from his teacher. It suggested that his parents take him out of school because he was holding back the entire class. The note said that the boy was "too stupid to learn."

When the boy's mother read the note she felt terrible. But she also felt challenged. She said, "My son, Tom, is *not* 'too stupid to learn.' I will teach him myself." And she did.

When Tom died many years later at the age of 84, the entire nation honored him in a remarkable way. At exactly 9:59 p.m., Eastern Standard Time, every home in the United States turned off its lights for one minute, as a tribute to the man who had invented those lights, Thomas Edison.

When the genius inventor died, a man who had been labeled as "too stupid to learn" in his younger years, he had over a thousand patents to his name including the lightbulb, the record player, the typewriter, and the motion picture movie projector. He even received the Congressional Medal of Honor.

MARK LINK and BRIAN CAVANAUGH

Wrestling Victory from Defeat

Let men label you as they may.

MARK TWAIN

Frank Whittle, inventor of the jet engine, showed his plans to the Professor of Aeronautical Engineering at Cambridge University who told him, "Very interesting, Whittle, my boy, but it will never work."

Singing legend Ray Charles was told by his music teacher: "You can't play the piano, and God knows you can't sing. You'd better learn how to weave chairs so you can support yourself."

Malcolm Forbes, founder of *Forbes* magazine, failed to make the staff of his school newspaper. He was rejected.

When news anchor Katie Couric began her television career, the president of CNN told her he never wanted to see her on camera again.

Fred Smith, founder of Fed Ex, was graded a "C" on his term paper at Yale University where he outlined his business plan for a reliable overnight delivery service.

Rudyard Kipling hoped to become a writer but was rejected by the *San Francisco Examiner* newspaper early in his career. He sent the editor of the paper samples of his work in 1889, and the response he received back read: "I'm sorry, Mr. Kipling, but you just don't know how to use the English language." Kipling went on to become a master of literature.

Beethoven's music teacher had little optimism for him and even remarked: "As a composer you are hopeless."

Woody Allen was given failing grades in both of the motion picture production classes he enrolled in during college. Despite this, he went on to become an Academy Award winning writer, producer, and director.

Actress and talk show host Rosie O'Donnell was told by her drama professor at Boston University that she lacked talent to become an actress.

Ted Turner introduced his plan for CNN and network officials rejected his idea, telling him: "A twenty-four hour news network will never work."

Abraham Lincoln entered the Blackhawk War as a captain, but by the end of the war he had been demoted to the rank of a private by his commanding officers.

Elvis Presley's high school music teacher graded him a "C" for his average ability.

Hollywood superstar Marlon Brando was constantly misbehaving in his younger years. His high school principal told him: "You'll never do anything with your life but dig ditches."

Talk show host mega-star Oprah Winfrey was demoted from her news job at WJZ-TV and was told that she "wasn't fit for television."

Actors Dustin Hoffman and Gene Hackman attended the same acting school. Both were voted by their classmates as "Least Likely to Succeed"—and both went on to become blockbuster stars in the movie industry.

The first nine records recorded by Diana Ross and the Supremes were all flops—complete failures. But the group refused to give up. Their tenth record, "Where Did Our Love Go," took them to the top of the charts, and to the top of the world.

Believe in yourself and there will come a day when others will have no choice but to believe with you.

CYNTHIA KERSEY

Life is not about how hard you can hit. It's about how hard you can get hit and keep moving forward.

SYLVESTER STALLONE

They Got Fired!

Keep putting one foot in front of the other even if you have to limp to do it.

JOAN RIVERS

Rush Limbaugh, the most listened to radio commentator in America, was fired from seven broadcasting jobs. He also quit college his freshman year after receiving failing grades in both of the speech classes he was enrolled in.

Composer Wolfgang Amadeus Mozart was fired as Concert Master in Salzburg, Austria.

Talk show host Regis Philbin was fired from KCOP-TV.

Top box-office draw Humphrey Bogart was fired from his job of reading laxative commercials.

Inventor genius Thomas Edison was fired from his job at the railroad where he sold newspapers and candy. He was also fired from four different telegraph operator jobs he held. His co-workers nicknamed him "The Looney," and one of his employers commented that Edison would probably "never amount to much."

Hollywood heartthrob Marilyn Monroe was fired from 20th Century Fox by production manager Darryl Zanuch because she was "unattractive."

Entertainer Frank Sinatra, a top-performing artist for over fifty years, was fired from his radio job.

Peter Benchley, author of *Jaws*, was fired as a speechwriter for Richard Nixon.

Bob Saget, host of *America's Funniest Home Videos*, was fired from hosting CBS's *The Morning Program*.

36. Be the kind of person who in the face of adversity will continue to embrace life and walk fearlessly toward the challenge. Take it on! Own your own power and glory!

OPRAH WINFREY

He who cannot endure the bad will never live to see the good.

YIDDISH PROVERB

37. Honor your challenges because the spaces you label as dark are actually there to bring you more light.

SANAYA ROMAN

What appears to be the end of the road may simply be a bend in the road.

ROBERT SCHULLER

38. Understand that the harder your conflict, the more glorious your triumph. What you obtain too cheaply, you will esteem too lightly.

THOMAS PAINE

Who has never tasted what is bitter does not know what is sweet.

GERMAN PROVERB

39. Always remember that the most massive characters are seared with scars. Out of suffering have emerged the strongest souls.

EDWIN CHAPIN

The purest ore is produced from the hottest furnace.

CHARLES CALEB COLTON

40. Carefully observe which way your heart draws you, and then choose that way with all of your strength.

HASIDIC PROVERB

Listening to your heart is not simple. Finding out who you are is not simple. It takes a lot of hard work and courage to get to know who you are and what you want.

SUE BENDER

Did you know?

Sally Jesse Raphael, host of the two-time Emmy Award winning television program, The Sally Jesse Raphael Show, *was fired eighteen times in the broadcasting industry, and often slept in her car, before she landed the position that became her life's passion for the next nineteen years.*

Aspire Higher

We know the story, the childhood favorite about a little railroad steam engine that encountered a great mountain along its way and was unable to go on. The steam engine wouldn't go on because it believed it couldn't go on. It thought the mountain was too high, and it thought itself too little. And as long as the steam engine believed this, it was true.

So there the engine stayed, on the tracks below the mountain, staring up to the peak from down below, afraid, until it got to thinking that the summit could be reached if only he tried. Four words later, the wheels below him started turning. Those words were: "I think I can."

This belief moved the little locomotive upward and set his engine to roaring, propelling him over the mountain and into the world beyond. The little steam engine thought he could, and so he did. He believed, and so he achieved.

We, too, can reach for the summits of our life and fulfill our dreams, but before we can achieve, we must first believe.

Never doubt for a single second that your dreams are reachable. You can reach them because they lie within your own heart.

Here, within our hearts, we also encounter our mountains—mountains of fear and doubt that would convince us otherwise. Just as positive thinking is a power, so is fear. And the time comes when each of us must decide what it is we will be made of. We hold the power to choose to believe in the mountains that stand in our way or in the miracle that is waiting to be our life. Which will it be?

There is a world that awaits us on the other side of self-doubt, a world that only we can take ourselves to. When we come against our fears with the power of positive faith and positive hope, these mountains cease to be victorious over us and we discover that they're not so big after all.

What is it you hope for? What is it you dream? Today, spend a few moments thinking about your answers to these questions. Then carefully examine your thoughts regarding your dreams. Do you find yourself more often believing "I can't do it" or believing the opposite perspective of "Yes, I can!"? Pay close attention to your thoughts. It is worth your while to do so because your perspective directly and profoundly influences the realization of everything you hope for. The world you determine to build around you is first built within. We live our lives from the inside out—every single one of us. We may have different dreams from one another, different destinations to arrive at, but we travel the same path on our way to them, the pathway through our heart. And along this path we come to realize that the only obstacle that can ever stand in our way is ourselves.

Know this: There isn't a place in the whole wide world that someone else can go to that you cannot. There isn't a dream your heart is hoping for that someone else can achieve and you will be denied. Do you believe this? It matters if you do. It matters very much.

A great promise was delivered to mankind two thousand years ago and the promise was this: "All things are possible to him who believes." The message was not "some" things, and it was not "many" things. The message was "all." All things are possible. Possible for who? Possible for the one who believes. Is this you?

When your answer becomes "yes," you will know it—and others will, too. They will hear in your voice and see in your eyes that the engine of hope has started to roar in your soul.

Then, there will be but one thing left for you to do—fasten your seatbelt because you're about to head straight up the side of a mountain.

ROCHELLE PENNINGTON

What is opportunity, and when does it knock? It never knocks. You can wait a whole lifetime, listening, hoping, and you will hear no knocking—none at all. *You* are opportunity, and you must knock on the door leading to your destiny.

MAXWELL MALTZ

41. Never forget that accomplishments come to the person who says: "I can make it happen."

BRIAN CAVANAUGH

You can take a man and measure him, examine him, analyze him, and dissect his statistics, but you cannot look into his heart. That's where the thirst is—the hunger. That's where desire turns to fire.

M. L. CARR

42. Do not seesaw between believing in your ability and doubting in it, quarreling with yourself. It is a type of civil war.

CHARLES CALEB COLTON

A house divided against itself cannot stand.

MARK 3:25

43. Always remember that every human being has a work to carry on within, duties to perform, influence to exert, which are peculiarly his, and which no conscience but his own can teach.

WILLIAM ELLERY CHANNING

To be nobody but yourself in a world which is doing its best, day and night, to make you like everybody else is to fight the hardest battle which any human being can fight.

E. E. CUMMINGS

Did you know?

World-famous artist Pablo Picasso was terrible at mathematics when he was a boy because every time he saw the number "4"" he visualized a nose instead of a number, and then he drew a portrait around it

If a man does not keep pace with his companions, perhaps it is because he hears a different drummer. Let him step to the music that he hears, however measured or far away.

HENRY DAVID THOREAU

Let Your Dreams Take Flight

"It is the greatest shot of adrenaline to be doing what you've wanted to do so badly. You almost feel as if you could fly without the plane."

CHARLES LINDBERGH, AVIATOR

44. When you're pretty sure that an adventure is going to happen, brush the honey off your nose and spruce yourself up as best as you can so you look ready for anything.

WINNIE THE POOH

The big question is whether you are going to say a hearty "YES!" to your adventure.

JOSEPH CAMPBELL

45. Always remember that you are never given a dream without also having been given the power to make it come true.

RICHARD BACH

You must have faith in one's mission—in the conviction that the creator has given each of us power to realize our life call, as it is written in our blood and stamped on our brain cells.

ORISON SWETT MARDEN

Real power is when you are doing exactly what you know you are supposed to be doing, the best it can be done. Authentic power. There's a surge, there's a kind of energy field that says, "I'm in my groove, I'm in my groove." And nobody has to tell you, "You go, girl," because you know you're already gone.

OPRAH WINFREY
Commencement Address to the Graduates
of Salem College, North Carolina

When your heart is in your dream, no request is too extreme.

JIMINY CRICKET

The Kid Stays in the Picture

Children have one special quality that gives them a far greater power than adults. They have imagination. They still think they can fly. They even think they can talk to prime ministers as equals.

CRAIG KIELBURGER

He was no scholar, and his classmates teased him. Rather than read, the kid really preferred running around with an 8 mm camera, shooting homemade movies of wrecks of his Lionel train set (which he showed to friends for a small fee).

In his sophomore year of high school, he dropped out. But when his parents persuaded him to return, he was mistakenly placed in a learning-disabled class. He lasted one month. Only when the family moved to another town did he land in a more suitable high school, where he eventually graduated.

After being denied entrance into a traditional filmmaking school, Steven Spielberg enrolled in English at California State College at Long Beach. Then in 1965, he recalls, in one of those serendipitous moments, his life took a complete turn. Visiting Universal Studios, he met Chuck Silvers, an executive in the editorial department. Silvers like the kid who made 8 mm films and invited him back sometime to visit.

Spielberg appeared the next day. Without a job or security clearance, he (dressed in a dark suit and tie, carrying his father's briefcase with nothing inside but "a sandwich and candy bars") strode confidently up to the guard at the gate of Universal and gave him a casual wave. The guard waved back. He was in.

"For an entire summer," Spielberg remembers, "I dressed in my suit and hung out with the directors and writers (including Silvers, who knew the kid wasn't a studio employee, but winked at the deception). I even found an office that wasn't being used, and became a squatter. I bought some plastic tiles and put my name in the building directory: Steven Spielberg, Room 23C."

It paid off for everyone. Ten years later, the 28-year-old Spielberg directed *Jaws*, which took in $470 million, then the highest-grossing movie of all time. Dozens of films and awards have followed because Steven Spielberg knew what his teachers didn't—talent is in the eyes of the filmmaker.

FRAN LOSTYS

Failing His Way to Success

Working in the control room of the salvage vessel *Seaprobe* at two o'clock one morning in 1977, Robert Ballard was jolted by a massive piece of equipment that crashed onto the deck just three feet above him. The ship shook with the force of an explosion. A drill pipe and its attached pod, full of sonar and video gear, had snapped and plunged into the Atlantic Ocean, abruptly ending the explorer's test run to find the *Titanic*.

"I lost a lot of credibility with sponsors, who had loaned the $600,000 worth of equipment for the 1977 expedition," said Ballard. "It took me eight years to recover from that." But recover he did, despite skepticism from other scientists, failed fund-raising efforts, and other setbacks. After the *Seaprobe* debacle, Ballard says, "I was back to square one. I had to come up with another way to search for the *Titanic*."

He returned to active duty as a U.S. Navy officer assigned to intelligence. At a time when the Cold War was still being waged, the marine geologist cut a deal with Navy officials. He would offer his expertise if they would fund the development and testing of Argo, a camera-equipped underwater robot critical to the *Titanic* mission, and allow him to use it for exploration.

The Navy sent Ballard and Argo on classified missions to survey *Thresher* and *Scorpion*, two nuclear submarines that sank during the 1960s. Those vessels lay in waters not far from the *Titanic*. After surveying the *Scorpion* in 1985, Ballard began looking for the doomed luxury liner. And two miles down, in the dark sea, he found it.

The oceanographer, who later found the German battleship *Bismark*, the liner *Lusitania*, and other historic wrecks, has a simple philosophy: "Failure and success are bedfellows, so I'm ready to fail."

JANICE LEARY

46. Remember that the future belongs to those who believe in the beauty of their dreams.

ELEANOR ROOSEVELT

When I look into the future, it's so bright, it burns my eyes.

OPRAH WINFREY

47. If you don't have a dream, how are you gonna make a dream come true?

From the movie *SOUTH PACIFIC*

We each have the power in our own hands to create the miracle of becoming the person we were meant to be.

JOE TYE

48. Knock the "t" off of "can't."

GEORGE REEVES

My doctors told me I would never walk again. My mother told me I would. I believed my mother.

WILMA RUDOLPH,
Named the "Fastest Woman in the World"
after breaking three world records for running

49. Be a "how" thinker, not an "if" thinker.

ANONYMOUS

Marathoner Joan Benoit underwent knee surgery only seventeen days before the U. S. Olympic trials, but her determination enabled her not only to make the team, but also to win the first ever Olympic gold medal in her event.

ROGER VAN OECH

50. Remember that the person who says something can't be done is often interrupted by someone doing it.

HARRY FOSDICK

The Bible says that all things are possible. I believe that.

DOLLY PARTON

51. Take the word "impossible" out of your dictionary.

HENRY FORD

I believe I am made in the image and likeness of my creator, who gave me a burning desire, a measure of talent, and a strong faith to attempt the difficult and to overcome the seemingly impossible.

WILLIAM ARTHUR WARD

What is "Impossible"?

Just because something hasn't been done before, doesn't mean that it can't be done.

TED HOOD

Since the days of ancient Greece, for thousands of years, humans have believed that it was impossible to run a mile in less than four minutes. Then one day, a man named Roger Bannister proved that the doctors, the trainers, and the athletes themselves were all wrong when he ran a mile in record time.

And, miracles of miracles, the year after Bannister broke the four-minute mile, thirty-seven other runners broke it, too. And only one year after that, 300 more runners accomplished the feat because the illusion of "impossible" had been removed from their minds.

HARVEY MACKAY

52. Consider the observation of Napoleon Hill who said: "When your desire to achieve your goal becomes strong enough you will appear to possess superhuman powers."

Some men have thousands of reasons why they cannot do what they want to do, when all they need is one reason why they can.

WILLIE R. WHITNEY

53. Practice mustard seed faith and positive thinking, and remarkable things will start to happen.

SIR JOHN WALTON

If you have faith as small as a mustard seed... nothing will be impossible for you.

MATTHEW 17:20-21

54. Decide what it is that you want in every area of your life. Imagine it vividly. Then act on your desire by actually constructing your personal goal book. There are no impossible dreams. And remember, God has promised to give His children the desires of their heart.

GLENNA SALSBURY

Trust in the Lord and do good... Delight yourself in the Lord and He will give you the desires of your heart. Commit your way to the Lord; trust in Him and He will do this.

PSALM 37:5

55. Understand that someday all you'll have to light your way will be a single ray of faith—and it will be enough.

KOBI YAMADA

Faith is to believe what we do not see; the reward of faith is to see what we believe.

SAINT AUGUSTINE

Congratulations!
Today is your day!
You're off to great places!
You're off and away!
You have brains in your head,
You have feet in your shoes.
You can steer yourself
Any direction you choose.

DR. SEUSS

From a Hotel Swimming Pool to the Olympics

The size of your life will be determined by the size of your plans.

CHRISTINA FORTE

In the 2000 Summer Olympics in Sydney, an unlikely hero emerged. I'm talking about Eric Moussambani, a swimmer from Equatorial Guinea. Eric began the sport just nine months before the games. His dream was to enter the Olympics as a swimming contestant for his country. The only problem was that Eric had no access to water for training except in a small hotel swimming pool. In fact, his biggest concern during a television interview he gave seemed to be whether he could finish his race, which would be the longest distance he had ever swum in his life.

When the time came for him to swim in his assigned qualifying heat, the two other swimmers in the heat were both disqualified for false starts. So Eric swam the whole race alone in the pool to the wild cheers of hundreds of spectators.

What great performance brought out such excitement, enthusiastic support, and even a standing ovation from the international crowd? The swimmer's time was nearly twice that of the fastest qualifying time of the day. The swimmer was even slower than the record for the event that is twice as long as his. There was no question that he failed to win the event and, to be quite frank, failed badly. But there also was no question that Eric Moussambani was a large success in *trying*, and the fans let him know this in loud, supportive cheers. These cheers, he believed, enabled him to hang in there, endure, and finish the longest and most grueling swimming race of his life, the 100-meter freestyle (a mere two lengths of the pool).

CHARLES MANZ

Did you know?

When Paul Kephart, a World War II veteran who lost both legs in France, returned his artificial limbs to the manufacturer for repairs, the firm was astonished by them. The bolts were loose and the joints were badly worn.

An executive from the firm called to find out what on earth Kephart had done to cause such wear.

"Maybe it was the bowling that did it," Kephart said sheepishly, thinking of his average score of 160 in his league, "or perhaps it was playing basketball." Pausing for a moment, Kephart then added, "No, on second thought, it probably was from kicking a football around. I shouldn't have done that."

SALES UPBEAT

"I can't do it" never yet accomplished anything, but "I will try" has wrought wonders.

GEORGE P. BURNHAM

56. Reach high, for stars lie hidden in your soul. Dream deep, for every dream precedes the goal.

PAMELA VAULL STARR

The very least you can do in your life is figure out what you hope for. And the most you can do is live inside that hope. Not admire it from a distance, but live right in it, under its roof.

BARBARA KINGSOLVER

57. Always remember that nothing happens unless first a dream.

CARL SANDBURG

Some men see things and say, "Why?" But I dream things that never were, and say, "Why not?"

GEORGE BERNARD SHAW

Would you get into a taxi and tell the cabby, "Drive anywhere"? Would you wander onto the first plane you saw at the airport gate without bothering to ask where it's flying to? Of course not!! Yet it's amazing how unfocused we can be about the biggest asset we have—our lives.

DEBORAH ROSADO SHAW

58. Understand that the greatest power you possess is the power to choose.

J. MARTIN KOHE

Men are great only if they are determined to be so.

CHARLES DE GUALLE

59. Give consideration to the fact that your decisions will determine your destiny.

FREDERICK SPEAKMAN

You are where you are right now in your life because of the choices you have made and the actions you have taken. If you want to change your life, remember that change starts with you.

JEFFREY KELLER

Did you know?

John Johnson founded three magazine publications for blacks and written about blacks, including Ebony, *but it wasn't an easy task to accomplish. No one thought such a magazine would sell except Johnson.*

Despite a lack of support for his idea, Johnson went forward with his dream, borrowing $500 for printing the first issue and using his mother's furniture as collateral. When the first copy of Negro Digest *was finally published on November 1, 1942, no one wanted to sell it. Every distributor of magazines and newspapers refused to order the publication for their racks.*

Not to be defeated, Johnson asked all of his friends and family members to go to every newsstand they could find and ask to buy a copy of "that new magazine, Negro Digest.*"*

It didn't take long for the phone to start ringing with orders.

60. Twenty years from now you will be more disappointed by the things that you didn't do than by the ones you did do. So sail away from the safe harbor! Catch the trade winds in your sails! Explore! Dream! Discover!

MARK TWAIN

There are people who put their dreams in a little box and say, "Yes, I've got dreams, of course, I've got dreams." Then they put the box away and bring it out once in a while and look in it, and yep, they're still there. These are great dreams, but they never even get out of the box. It takes an uncommon amount of guts to put your dreams on the line, to hold them up and say, "How good or how bad am I?" That's where the courage comes in.

ERMA BOMBECK

61. Don't be afraid your life will end. Be afraid that it will never begin.

GRACE HANSEN

It's never too late to be what you might have been.

GEORGE ELIOT

How Old is Too Old?

World-famous pianist Arthur Rubinstein gave one of his greatest recitals at age 89.

Actress Jessica Tandy won an Academy Award for her role in the movie *Driving Miss Daisy* when she was 80 years old.

Environmentalist Marjory Stoneman Douglas was still actively championing the cause of preserving the Florida Everglades when she was 100.

Tintoretto, the great 16th century Renaissance artist, painted "Paradise"—a canvas measuring 74 feet by 30 feet!—when he was 74. Another great Renaissance artist, Titian, painted his historic scene of the "Battle of Lepanto" when he was 98 years old.

Jazz pianist/composer Eubie Blake was still performing at age 100.

Dr. Albert Schweitzer continued surgical operations in Africa at age 89.

Benjamin Franklin assisted with framing the U.S. Constitution at age 81.

Inventor Henry Ford kept both his mind and body physically fit throughout his life. He could still do handstands at age 75.

George Burns won his only Oscar at the advanced age of 80. He continued starring in Hollywood roles for another twenty years after that.

Circus performer Karl Wallenda continued to perform on tightropes suspended between high-rise skyscrapers at age 75.

Artist Pablo Picasso painted until he was in his 90's, and Grandma Moses continued her painting career until she was 100 years old. (Grandma Moses, the celebrated American artist, didn't begin painting until she was 78 years old—*and never even had an art lesson!*)

Goethe, the German writer, completed his masterpiece "Faust," when he was 80, and Tennyson, the 19th century English writer who made profound contributions to world literature throughout his lifetime, wrote "Crossing the Bar" when he was 83 years old.

Oliver Wendell Holmes, the American poet, novelist, and physician, wrote "Over the Teacups" at age 79.

Golda Meir became Prime Minister of Israel at 71.

Verdi gave the world his famous "Ave Maria" when he was 85.

When someone told 89-year-old poet Dorothy Duncan that she had lived a full life, she responded, "Don't you past-tense me! I am *living* a full life!"

62. Try to keep your soul young right up to old age, and to imagine right up to the brink of death that life is only beginning. In this way you will keep adding to your talent, your affections, and to your inner happiness.

GEORGE SAND

Asked which of his works he would select as his masterpiece, architect Frank Lloyd Wright said, "My next one." He was 83.

63. Dream dreams.

JOEL 2:28

To be truthful and honest and frank about it, the thing I would like to be right now is an astronaut.

CASEY STENGEL,
Quoted at age 83

64. Know where you are going. If you don't know where you are going, how do you expect to get there?

BASIL WALSH

The trouble with not having a goal is that you can spend all of your time running up and down the field of life and never score.

BILL COPELAND

65. Remember that people can be divided into three groups: Those who make things happen, those who watch things happen, and those who wonder what happened.

JOHN W. NEWBERN

The tragedy of life does not lie in not reaching your goal. The tragedy lies in not having a goal to reach.

BENJAMIN E. MAYS

66. Be decisive concerning your goal and be willing to make decisions. Don't fall victim to the "Ready-Aim-Aim-Aim Syndrome."

T. BOONE PICKENS

There comes a moment when you have to stop revving up the car and shove it into gear.

DAVID MAHONEY

67. Do you know why adults are always asking little kids what they want to be when they grow up? It's because they are looking for ideas.

PAULA POUNDSTONE

I've always wanted to be somebody, but I see now that I should have been more specific.

LILY TOMLIN

Let the Music Out

There comes that mysterious meeting in life when someone acknowledges who we are and all that we can be, igniting within us the circuits of our highest potential.

RUSTY BERKUS

Three neighborhood boys, Salvator, Julio, and Antonio, lived and played in Cremona, Italy, around the mid-1600s. Salvator had a beautiful tenor voice and Julio played the violin in accompaniment as they strolled the piazzas. Antonio also liked music and would have loved to sing along, but his voice squeaked like a creaky door hinge. All the children made fun of him whenever he tried to sing. Yet Antonio was not without talent. His most prized possession was the pocketknife his grandfather had given him. He was always whittling away on some piece of wood. In fact, Antonio made some very nice things with his whittling.

As the time for the annual festival approached, the houses and streets gradually became festooned with beautiful decorations for spring. Dressed in their finest clothes, people filled the streets. On festival day, Salvator and Julio planned to go to the cathedral where they would play and sing in the crowded plaza.

"Would you like to come with us?" they called to Antonio, who sat on his stoop whittling on a piece of wood. "Who cares if you can't sing. We'd like to have you come with us anyway."

"Sure, I'd like to come along," Antonio replied. "The festival is so much fun."

The three boys went off to the cathedral. As they walked along, Antonio kept thinking about their remark about his not being able to sing. It made him cry in his heart, because he loved music as much as they did, even if his voice did squeak a little.

When they arrived at the plaza, Julio began to play the violin while Salvator sang with his melodious voice. People stopped to listen, and most of them left a coin or two for the shabbily dressed boys. An elderly man stepped out from the crowd. He complimented them and placed a shiny coin into Salvator's hand. He then turned away and was quickly lost in the milling crowd.

Salvator opened his hand and gasped. "Look!" he shouted. "It's a gold coin." He clenched it between his teeth to make sure. All three boys were excited and passed the coin back and forth, examining it. They all agreed that it was a real gold piece.

"But he can well afford it," said Julio. "You know, he's the great Amati."

Antonio asked sheepishly, "And who is Amati? Why is he so great?"

Both boys laughed as they said, "You've never heard of Amati?"

"Of course he hasn't," said Julio. "He knows nothing about music makers. He has a squeaky voice and is just a whittler of wood." Julio went on, "For your information, Antonio, Amati happens to be a great violin maker, probably the best in all of Italy, or even the entire world, and he even lives here in our city."

As Antonio walked home that evening, his heart was very heavy. It seemed that he had been laughed at too often for his squeaky voice and his whittling. So, very early the next morning, Antonio left his home, carrying his precious whittling knife. His pockets were stuffed with some of the things he had made—a pretty bird, a flute, several statues, and a small boat. He was determined to find the home of the great Amati.

Eventually, Antonio found the house and gently knocked on the front door. When a servant opened it, the great master heard Antonio's squeaky voice and came to see what he wanted so early in the morning.

"I brought these for you to see, sir," replied Antonio, as he emptied his pockets of the assortment of items that he had carved. "I hope you will look at these and tell me if I have enough talent to learn how to make violins, too."

Amati carefully picked up and examined each piece, and invited Antonio into his house. "What is your name?" he asked.

"Antonio, sir," he said.

"And why do you want to make violins," inquired Amati, now quite serious.

Impulsively Antonio blurted, "Because I love music, but I cannot sing because my voice sounds like a creaky door hinge. You heard my talented friends singing when you were in front of the cathedral yesterday. I, too, want to make music come alive."

Leaning forward and looking Antonio in the eyes, Amati said, "The thing that matters most is the song in the heart. There are many ways of making music. Some people play the violin, others sing, still others paint wonderful pictures. Each helps to add to the splendor of the world. You are a whittler, but your song shall be as noble as any."

These words made Antonio very happy, and he never forgot this message of hope. In a very short while, Antonio became a student of the great artist. Very early, every morning, he went to Amati's workshop, where he listened and learned and watched his teacher. After many years, there was not one secret about the making of a violin, with all of its seventy different parts, that he did not know. By the time he was twenty-two years old, his master allowed him to put his own name on a violin he had made.

For the rest of his life, Antonio Stradivari made violins—more that 1,100 of them—trying to make each one better and more beautiful than the one before. Anyone who owns a Stradivarius violin (among the most valuable instruments in the world today) owns a treasure, a masterpiece of art.

We may not be able to sing, play, whittle, or make a violin, but if we really want to, we will find a way to let the music out of our hearts—whatever that music is.

SEEDS FROM THE SOWER

68. Remember that your "I can" is more important than your "IQ."

H. JACKSON BROWN

If we did all the things we are capable of doing, we would literally astound ourselves.

THOMAS EDISON

69. All that is, or ever shall be, is but reverberations and repercussions of this first thunderclap: "I WILL." It is both a declaration and a command. It affirms dominion. Take a moment and whisper it to yourself. "I WILL." Feel the power.

SUSAN L. TAYLOR

Alice laughed. "There's no use trying," she said. "One can't believe impossible things."

"I daresay you haven't had much practice," said the Queen. "When I was your age, I always did it for half an hour a day. Why, sometimes, I've believed as many as six impossible things before breakfast."

LEWIS CARROLL
Alice in Wonderland

I'm stirred when someone says, "You can't do it." I find the statement "you can't" offensive to the human spirit. We can be anything. Maybe this entire experience is a series of lessons to learn that you can—yes, you can.

MAYA ANGELOU

Believe. Receive.

STELLA TERRILL

70. Be bold, and mighty forces will come to your aid.

BASIL KING

The moment one definitely commits oneself, then heaven moves, too. All sorts of things occur to help that would never otherwise have happened. A stream of events issues from the decision, raising unforeseen incidents, meetings, and material assistance, which no man could have dreamt would have come his way.

W. H. MURRAY

71. Have faith in yourself and in your goal. It is an inward reservoir of courage, hope, confidence, calmness, and assuring trust that all will come out well—even though to the world it may appear that things will come out most badly.

B. C. FORBES

Simply to ask a blessing upon one's circumstances, whatever they are, is somehow to improve them, and to tap some mysterious source of energy. It is one of the most ancient and universal truths—that to affirm and to claim God's help even before it is given, is to receive it.

MARJORIE HOLMES

72. Never forget that no man is born into this world whose work is not born with him.

JAMES RUSSELL LOWELL

Put your ear down next to your soul and listen hard.

ANNE SEXTON

73. Understand that we all have the extraordinary coded within us waiting to be released.

JEAN HOUSTON

When Mozart, at age two and a half, heard a pig squeal outside his window, he responded by saying, "G sharp."

74. Fall in love with the magnificent possibilities within yourself.

MARIANNE WILLIAMSON

Glorious indeed is the world of God around us, but more glorious still is the world of God within us.

HENRY WADSWORTH

75. Always remember that you are a child of God. Your playing small does not serve the world. We are born to make manifest the glory of God that is within us. It is not just in some of us; it is in everyone.

NELSON MANDELA

The kingdom of God is within you.

LUKE 17:21

76. Do not go where the path may lead. Go instead where there is no path and leave a trail.

RALPH WALDO EMERSON

Two roads diverged in a woods, and I, I took the one less traveled by, and that has made all the difference.

ROBERT FROST

77. Forget committees. New, noble, world-changing ideas always come from one person working alone.

H. JACKSON BROWN

A committee should consist of six men, five of whom should be absent.

SIR HERBERT BEERBOHM TREE

Those who travel unworn paths find the rarest flowers.

INDIAN PROVERB

Overcoming Obstacles and Failure

"How a person masters his fate is more important than what his fate is."

WILHELM VON HUMBOLDT

78. Always remember that failure is delay, not defeat. It is a temporary detour, not a dead-end street.

WILLIAM ARTHUR WARD

I quit being afraid when my first venture failed and the sky didn't fall down.

ALLEN H. NEUHARTH

79. Understand that success is determined by how you deal with failure.

DAVID FEHERTY

You must have long-range goals to keep you from being frustrated by short-term failures.

CHARLES NOBLE

If you find a path with no obstacles on it, chances are it doesn't lead anywhere.

ANONYMOUS

Lincoln's Road to the White House

When fate knocks us flat on our back, there is no place to look but up.

ROBERT BABSON

Born in a one-room log cabin, 1809. Lincoln walked nine miles to school every day each way.

Failed in business, 1831. It took many years to pay off these debts.

Defeated for legislature, 1832.

Second failure in business, 1833.

Defeated for speaker, 1838.

Defeated for elector, 1840.

Defeated for congress, 1843.

Defeated for congress again, 1848.

Defeated for senate, 1855.

Defeated for vice president, 1856.

Defeated for senate again, 1858.

Elected President of the United States of America, 1860.

80. Give consideration to the fact that courage doesn't always roar. Sometimes courage is the quiet voice at the end of the day saying, "I will try again tomorrow."

MARY ANNE RADMACHER-HERSHEY

"Everyday courage" has few witnesses, but yours is no less noble because no drum beats before you and no crowds shout your name.

ROBERT LOUIS STEVENSON

81. When everything seems to be going against you, remember that the airplane takes off against the wind, not with it.

HENRY FORD

Every challenge we are presented with when we pursue our dreams provides us with an opportunity to seize a gift of power. Sounds mysterious, eh? Every time you face a challenge, you are being tested as to how strong your beliefs and intentions are. People who go through great hardships to achieve greatness have a kind of aura about them that says, "Don't mess with me, I know what I'm about. I have been thoroughly tested in battle." Confront your challenges with a brave face. The greater the challenge the greater the gift of power.

A. C. PING

82. Ever tried? Ever failed? No matter. Try again. Fail again. Fail better.

SAMUEL BECKETT

When I was young I observed that nine out of ten things were failures so I did ten times more work.

GEORGE BERNARD SHAW

83. Recognize that most advances are made by mistake. You uncover what is when you get rid of what isn't.

BUCKMINSTER FULLER

Failure is simply the opportunity to begin again more intelligently.

HENRY FORD

I have always been delighted at the prospect of a new day, a fresh try, one more start, with perhaps a bit of magic waiting somewhere behind the morning.

J. B. PRIESTLY

Did you know?

Thomas Edison invented the light bulb after 2,000 experiments. When asked how he felt about his repeated failures he replied, "I never failed once. My invention just happened to be a 2,000 step process."

Edison's trial-and-error methodology, a painstakingly difficult process, often tempted his co-workers to give up. After 700 unsuccessful attempts during the light bulb experiment, Edison's assistant said to him, "We still don't have an answer. We have failed."

"No, my friend," responded Edison. "It's just that we know more about this subject than anyone alive. And we are closer to finding the answer because we now know 700 things not to do. Don't call it a failure. Call it an education."

84. Never forget that success is the result of preparation, hard work, and learning from failure.

COLIN POWELL

Failure is, in a sense, the highway to success, since every discovery of what is false leads us to seek earnestly after what is true.

JOHN KEATS

85. Profit from your losses.

WILLIAM BOLITHO

The happy and efficient people in this world are those who accept trouble as a normal detail of human life and resolve to capitalize on it when it comes along.

H. BERTRAM LEWIS

86. Always remember that there is only one thing more painful than learning from experience, and that is not learning from experience.

ARCHIBALD MACLEISH

A man who has committed a mistake and doesn't correct it is committing another mistake.

CONFUCIUS

87. Never be ashamed to admit you have made a mistake, which is but saying in other words that you are wiser today than you were yesterday.

ALEXANDER POPE

When we can begin to take our failures and difficulties non-seriously, it means we are ceasing to be afraid of them.

KATHERINE MANSFIELD

88. Learn from the mistakes of others. You can't live long enough to make them all yourself.

VANBEE

No one ever sized up humans more accurately than the fellow who invented the pencil eraser.

ANONYMOUS

89. Understand that you will learn some things best in calm, and some in storm.

WILLA CATHER

Experience is the most brutal of teachers. But you learn, by God, do you learn.

C. S. LEWIS

90. Remember that experience is a hard teacher. She gives you the test first, and the lesson afterwards.

ANONYMOUS

Success is the result of good judgment. Good judgment is the result of experience. Experience is the result of bad judgment.

ANTHONY ROBBINS

Did you know?

Billionaire Bill Gates has this definition of success: "Success is all about how you approach failure, and believe me, we at Microsoft know a lot about failure. In truth, the weight of all of our failures could easily cause me to be too depressed to come into work if I thought about our failures as problems. Instead, I am excited about their challenge and about how we can continue to learn how to use today's bad news to help solve tomorrow's problems. Once you embrace unpleasant news not as a negative, but as evidence of a need for change, you are no longer defeated by it—you're learning from it."

91. Never forget that the place which may seem like the end may also be only the beginning.

IVY BAKER PRIEST

Most people achieved their greatest success one step beyond what looked like their greatest failure.

BRIAN TRACY

92. Give consideration to the fact that it can be hard to tell your bad luck from your good luck sometimes; hard to tell for many years to come.

MERLE SHAIN

I think one of life's great milestones is when a person can look back and be almost as thankful for the setbacks as for the victories.

BOB DOLE

Did you know?

A tentmaker by the name of Strauss failed in business in the 1850s, but instead of giving up on the heavy-duty fabric he had invented, he decided to cut his tents apart and sew the material into pants. His signature "Levi" blue jeans transformed the fashion industry.

Scientists at the 3M Company invented an adhesive they believed was a failure because the glue refused to remain permanently adhered. One of their scientists, Art Fry, then discovered that the adhesive allowed paper to be attached and re-attached easily. His idea became Post-It Notes, 3-M's most successful product.

Julio Iglesias was a professional soccer player in Madrid when a car accident left him paralyzed for more than a year and destroyed his soccer career. To help Iglesias pass the time in the hospital, a nurse gave him a guitar. Although Iglesias had no prior musical plans, he went on to become one of the greatest music stars ever.

93. Press on! A better fate awaits you!

VICTOR HUGO

God always has another custard pie up His sleeve.

LYNN REDGRAVE

Did you know?

A young man, Robert L. Ripley, was enthusiastically entering upon a career in big-league baseball. However, after long months of practice, he broke his arm during the first game that he pitched. His career was over. Disappointed but not despondent, Ripley taught himself to draw. A job as a newspaper sports cartoonist afforded him preliminary training for what was to become a highly successful career. His word-pictures and penciled drawings brought him worldwide fame as "Mr. Believe It or Not," who unearthed more oddities than any other person in history. During the remainder of his life, Ripley continued to regard the fractured arm in his first major-league ballgame as the luckiest "break" he ever had.

BITS AND PIECES

94. Never forget that when one door closes, another opens; but we often look so long and so regretfully upon the closed door that we do not see the one which has opened for us.

ALEXANDER GRAHAM BELL

Change is the law of life. And those who look only to the past are certain to miss their future.

JOHN F. KENNEDY

95. Cremate your disappointments—don't embalm them.

HENRY S. HASKINS

Achievers have an attitude of expectancy. They minimize their losses. They do not grieve over failures or what might have been. Achievers look around the corner in anticipation of the good things that still await them.

ALLAN COX

Encountering Life's Hurdles....and Jumping Them

Adversity causes some men to break, and others to break records.

WILLIAM ARTHUR WARD

Two high school football teams from Michigan opposed one another first on the field, and then in the courtroom. The losing team took legal action to have the victory of their opponent reversed when they found out that one of the star players from the team had played with extra equipment, an unfair advantage. The judge heard the argument, and the victory stood. His determination? The artificial leg the player in question attached before the game was not only acceptable, it was commendable.

And speaking of football, who remembers the record setting 63-yard-field goal Tom Dempsey kicked in the game between the Detroit Lions and the New Orleans Saints in November of 1970? The kick in itself was amazing enough without knowing that Dempsey has no toes on his right foot and only half on his kicking foot.

And speaking of toes, a wonderful novel, *Down All the Days*, was published by a 37-year-old Irishman named Christy Brown.

And what does this have to do with toes?

Well, Mr. Brown just so happened to type the entire manuscript with the little one on his left foot. Brain damaged at birth, his vocal chords emitted only grunts, making it impossible for him to verbally dictate. He was also born without arms, unable to write out the manuscript. But what he lacked physically, he made up for in an area within his power—determination.

ROCHELLE PENNINGTON

Did you know?

Soichiro Honda, founder of Honda Motor Company, is a dramatic example of an alternative route to success. After growing up in an impoverished family in which several of his brothers and sisters died of starvation, Honda encountered dramatic setbacks in his professional life including the bombing of his original piston plant in 1945 during World War II and later the complete destruction of the factory by an earthquake.

CHARLES MANZ

96. Learn to accept finite disappointment, but never lose infinite hope.

MARTIN LUTHER KING, JR.

The greatest test of courage on earth is to bear defeat without losing heart.

ROBERT INGERSOLL

97. Make the most of all that comes and the least of all that goes.

SARA TEASDALE

The workshop of character is everyday life. The uneventful and common place hour is where the battle is lost or won.

MALTBIE BABCOCK

98. Memorize Coach Lou Holtz's observation: "Life is 10% what happens to us and 90% how we react to it."

I've seen kids on my baseball team go into a slump and never come out, and I've seen others snap right out and come back better than ever. I guess more players lick themselves than are ever licked by the opposing team.

CONNIE MACK

Did you know?

Claude Perrin (1644-1709), the noted French painter, found his right hand suddenly paralyzed at the age of 40. Instead of giving up, he taught himself to paint so well with his left hand that his later art works are his most valued.

Golf Balls and Butterflies Take Flight… and So Can We

What does the word "four" make you think of? The number after three?

I might think this, too—unless it's a beautiful day. Then I'd think of golf. "Fore," that is, yelled behind a bumpy, white ball soaring for a distant green.

Hard and dimpled, modern day golf balls no longer have their ancestors' original outer casing which was perfectly smooth, similar to a ping pong ball. The golf balls were re-made and "dimpled" when someone discovered that roughing them up a little made them fly further and faster.

Golf balls, humans. Same.

And speaking of flying… Have you ever watched a butterfly being born? The cocoon seems to convulse endlessly, convincing the onlooker that the butterfly is surely trapped and it will never break free. Any witness to such a delivery can be tempted to help—to just tear the cocoon wall ever so gently, making it easy for the butterfly to come through. Ironically, to do for the butterfly what the butterfly needs to do for itself is to deny it its ability to fly.

The process of struggle within the cocoon is what builds the strength the butterfly needs to soar. No struggle, no flight.

Butterflies, humans. Same.

ROCHELLE PENNINGTON

If there is one skill in life that each of us needs to learn it's how to get back up, dust ourselves off, and get on with things.

A. C. PING

Did you know?

Thomas Edison's laboratory complex in New Jersey was destroyed by fire in 1914. In one night, Edison lost two million dollars worth of equipment, as well as the records to most of his life's work.

While firemen battled the blaze, Edison was, surprisingly, far from distraught. He summoned his son to come see "the spectacular sight" and then told his son to get his mother. "She'll never see anything like this again as long as she lives," he said.

Edison got to work rebuilding the site immediately with a newer, more up-to-date facility. He was quoted as saying: "There is great value in disaster. All of our mistakes are burned up. Thank God, we can start anew!" It was an amazing reaction by an amazing man to what some would have viewed as a disastrous setback.

Character cannot be developed in ease and quiet. Only through experiences of trial and suffering can the soul be strengthened, vision cleared, ambition inspired, and success achieved.

HELEN KELLER

Turn Setbacks into Comebacks

Always know that you are far bigger than anything that can happen to you.

DAN ZADRA

Billionaire J. K. Rowlings, author of the *Harry Potter* books, was divorced, unemployed, and living on welfare in a mouse-infested apartment when she submitted her first manuscript in the series for consideration.

Ludwig van Beethoven wrote his greatest music after he was completely deaf.

President Franklin D. Roosevelt governed the United States of America for four terms from a wheelchair. He was paralyzed.

Statesman Winston Churchill, one of the greatest orators and speechwriters the world has known, suffered from severe depression which he called “the black dog that follows me everywhere.”

Thomas Monaghan, founder of Domino’s Pizza, grew up in orphanages and foster homes.

At the peak of Norman Rockwell’s career in 1943, a fire ravaged the famous painter’s studio and most of Rockwell’s original paintings, as well as historical costumes, props, and sketch books filled with ideas for future artwork, were destroyed. Despite "the enormous loss," Rockwell faced the devastation by working as hard as ever to recapture his work and ideas.

Poet John Milton, a literary genius—"second only to Shakespeare"—went blind at the age of forty-four but continued to produce great works afterward, some say his greatest.

Wealth baron Andrew Carnegie, "the second richest man in the world," started working in a cotton factory twelve hours a day, six days a week, at the young age of thirteen when his family arrived in America. Carnegie's parents were so "dirt poor" that they had to borrow money to emigrate.

Cycling extraordinaire Lance Armstrong was one of the top cyclists in the world in 1996. Then tragedy struck. He was diagnosed with testicle cancer and tumors spread to his lungs, abdomen, and brain. Doctors gave him a 40% chance of survival. Despite the grim diagnosis, Armstrong refused to surrender to the disease and fought his way through the cancer and then to the top of his profession, winning seven consecutive races in the Tour de France, the most grueling bicycle competition in the world.

Fall down seven times.
Stand up eight.

JAPANESE PROVERB

99. Never forget that a man of character finds a special attractiveness in difficulty, since it is only by coming to grips with difficulty that he can realize his potentialities.

CHARLES DE GUALLE

I do not choose to be a common man. I seek opportunity—not security. I want to take the calculated risk; to dream and to build, to fail and to succeed. I prefer the challenges of life to a guaranteed existence; the thrill of fulfillment to the stale of calm. It is my heritage to stand erect, proud, and unafraid; to think for myself, to enjoy the benefits of my creations, to face the world boldly, and to say, "This I have done."

DEAN ALFANGE

100. Remember that winners never quit, and quitters never win.

TED TURNER

I never tried quitting, and I never quit trying.

DOLLY PARTON

101. When things get rough, remember: It's the rubbing that brings out the shine.

E. C. McKENZIE

Unless a man has been kicked around a little, you can't really depend upon him to amount to anything.

WILLIAM FEATHER

102. Learn to embrace difficulty. The struggles of today are but the price you must pay for the accomplishments and victories of tomorrow.

WILLIAM BOETCKER

I would never have amounted to anything were it not for adversity. I was forced to come up the hard way.

J. C. PENNEY

Did you know?

NASA has used significant failure as an important criterion for selecting new recruits. When NASA was looking for potential astronauts for the Apollo 11 lunar mission, they invited resumes from the American public. They first weeded out applicants based on academic qualifications but they still had several thousand candidates.

The next step was a very interesting one. They weeded out all candidates who had not bounced back from a significant failure at some point in their career.

One might think it would be more logical to select those whose career performance was so strong that they had never experienced significant failure. They instead actually sought those who had failed. The apparent premise was that a person who had failed and then got up again was a stronger contender than one who had never experienced failure.

Perhaps the best way to view this seemingly radical thinking at NASA would be to conclude that they wanted astronauts who had developed sufficient inner strength to withstand challenge.

THE POWER OF FAILURE

Never Give Up

Failure is not falling down. Failure is not getting up.

ABRAHAM LINCOLN

Before writing *The Wonderful Wizard of Oz*, L. Frank Baum went bankrupt in a general store and also started a newspaper which subsequently went broke.

American poet Robert Frost, winner of the Pulitzer Prize, failed as a teacher and as a farmer.

President Harry Truman applied for entrance into the Military Academy at West Point and also into the Naval Academy at Annapolis during his younger years. He was rejected by both. He then opened a haberdashery business in Kansas City. It failed.

Henry Ford went broke several times before he succeeded in the automobile industry.

Apollo 12 astronaut Charles Conrad was an "F" student in his childhood school in Pennsylvania.

Actor William Shatner, *Star Trek's* Captain Kirk, was so poor after the *Star Trek* series on television was cancelled that he slept in a camper hitched to the back of his pick-up truck for several years. He regained fame and fortune when *Star Trek* was made into a hit movie.

Hollywood leading man Harrison Ford quit acting for a time and became a carpenter after his acting roles proved to be flops early in his career.

President Lyndon Johnson was kicked out of college and worked as an automobile mechanic.

Presidential candidate John McCain graduated 895th out of 900 students at the United States Naval Academy.

Patrick Henry—"Give me liberty or give me death"—failed as a storekeeper and as a farmer.

F. W. Woolworth's first store went bust.

President Woodrow Wilson opened a law office early in his career. It failed.

Academy Award winning songwriter E. Y. "Yip" Harburger, creator of *The Wizard of Oz's* "Over the Rainbow," "Ding Dong the Witch is Dead," and "If I Only Had a Brain," originally owned an appliance store which went bankrupt.

Movie star Sylvester Stallone's teachers didn't think he would amount to much because he "spent as much time in the principal's office as he did in the classroom." By the time Sylvester was 16 years old, he had been expelled from multiple different schools.

103. Give consideration to the fact that it takes as much courage to have tried and failed as it does to have tried and succeeded.

ANNE MORROW LINDBERGH

A word of encouragement during a failure is worth more than a whole book of praise after a success.

ANONYMOUS

Did you know?

In 1860, a thirty-eight year old man was working as a handyman for his father, a leather merchant. He kept books, drove wagons, and handled hides for about $66 a month.

Prior to this menial job, the man had failed as a soldier, a farmer, and a real estate agent. Most of the people who knew him had written him off as a failure.

Eight years later he was President of the United States. The man was Ulysses S. Grant.

BITS AND PIECES

How would you like a job where, if you made a mistake, a big red light would go on and 18,000 people would boo?

JACQUES PLANTE, hockey goalie

104. Forget the blunders of yesterday and make it a habit to live fully today.

MAXWELL MALTZ

Cyrus H. K. Curtis, of the old Saturday Evening Post, *used to keep a large sign hanging in his office which read, "Yesterday ended last night."*

105. Always remember that you can't have rosy thoughts about the future when your mind is full of blues about the past.

E. C. McKENZIE

If you let your past control your present you will never have a future.

SUZIE DAVIS

Fight one more round. When your feet are so tired that you have to shuffle back to the center of the ring, fight one more round. When your arms are so tired that you can hardly lift your hands to come on guard, fight one more round. When your nose is bleeding and your eyes are black and you are so tired that you wish your opponent would crack you one on the jaw and put you to sleep, fight one more round.

JAMES J. CORBETT, prize fighter

Give up? Quit now? No way!

The final pitch is thrown, the batter swings. Strike three. A discouraged little heart is about to return home where the decision will unfortunately be made to stay there. His baseball season has come to an early close, by choice.

There are few people, if any, who cannot relate to the pressing feeling of disappointment when our accomplishments fall short of our hopes.

But one needs to look no further than the all-time greatest baseball players to realize that failure is not "a falling down," but "a staying down."

Consider these two Hall of Fame heroes:

Babe Ruth held two records—one for the most home runs, and the other for the most strikeouts.

Ty Cobb, America's greatest all-time hitter, entered the Hall of Fame with a batting average of .367. That means that for every three times he swung the bat, only one resulted in a hit.

And these guys are the greatest!

106. Remember that you may have to fight a battle more than once to win it.

MARGARET THATCHER

Never give in! Never give in! Never, never, never, never!

WINSTON CHURCHILL

Did you know?

Walt Disney's first company, Laugh-O-Grams, went broke. He then lost his job at Rubin Commercial Art Studio because of lack of talent, in the company's opinion. His next company, Iwerks-Disney Commercial Artists, went bankrupt. Disney then restarted his earlier company, Laugh-O-Grams Films. It went bankrupt.

107. Understand that life is a grindstone, but whether you think it is grinding you down or polishing you up depends upon you.

L. THOMAS HOLDCROFT

The gem cannot be polished without friction, nor the man perfected without trials.

JAPANESE PROVERB

108. Face your challenges head on.

SCOTT MILTON

Hold your head high, stick your chest out. You can make it. It gets dark sometimes, but morning comes. Keep hope alive.

JESSE JACKSON

In Sun or Storm, Evergreens Endure

Only in winter can you tell which trees are truly green. Only when the winds of adversity blow can you tell whether an individual has courage and steadfastness.

JOHN F. KENNEDY

Twenty-one degrees. Not a particularly bad temperature forecast for wintertime in Wisconsin until the radio weatherman added those two extra little words—"below zero." Brrrrrrrrrr.

I watched out my kitchen window as the frigid cold moved across the countryside and challenged all in its path with numbing severity. Submission was evident. Evident, but not everywhere.

Amid the surrounding harshness stood the evergreens, firm and steadfast, with a constancy strengthened from within.

Evergreens. They're everywhere. Some of them have roots and trunks and branches; others have bodies and arms and legs.

Like Wilma Rudolph. Born prematurely in 1940 with polio, the 20th of 22 children, she was not expected to survive. But she did survive, only to contract scarlet fever, chicken pox, measles, double pneumonia, and mumps at age four. Most children would have died, but not Wilma. She lived through it, but was left paralyzed in her left leg. Those are the facts.

Despite them, eleven-year-old Wilma, determined not only to walk but to run, took her leg brace off and eventually was doing both—and very well at that. By 1956 she had an Olympic bronze medal hanging around her neck, and by the 1960 Rome Olympics she had three gold medals and three world records. Wilma is a winner in sports and in life, an evergreen among us.

So is Todd Hutson. Things weren't going so well for this young man either. First, Todd was involved in a boating accident. His legs were sucked into the engine's propeller and were severely mangled. Then, infection set in. Finally, his right leg had to be amputated—not good news for someone who loved sports and the physical challenge they presented.

But Todd Hutson refused to surrender to his injury and, instead, rose above it—literally. This one-legged fellow started climbing mountains, accomplishing feats greater than any he had experienced before his accident. And on August 7, 1994, he accomplished his greatest feat of all. On this day, Todd Hutson was standing on top of Mount Mauna Kea in Hawaii, having just climbed 50 mountains in 66 days (including Mt. McKinley in Alaska and Mt. Hood in Oregon). He shattered the previous world record by a remarkable 35 days—a record set by a climber in perfect health. Todd Hutson had triumphed against all odds and is an evergreen among us.

Evergreens. They're everywhere. Some of them have roots and trunks and branches; others have bodies and arms and legs.

ROCHELLE PENNINGTON

They Did What?!

If you have made mistakes, even serious ones, there is always another chance for you.

MARY PICKFORD

What do the following people have in common?

Actor John Travolta, fashion designer Liz Claiborne, songwriter-composer Irving Berlin, *American Idol* judge Simon Cowell, newspaper publisher Horace Greeley, actor Russell Crowe, singer-songwriter Elton John, author Mark Twain, singer Dean Martin, photographer Ansel Adams, America's first multi-millionaire John Jacob Astor, aviation engineer Orville Wright, designer-artist Gloria Vanderbilt, actor Tom Cruise, comedian Groucho Marx, playwright George Bernard Shaw, singer Celine Dion, magician Harry Houdini, actress-singer Cher, painter Vincent Van Gogh, poet Walt Whitman, country singer Tanya Tucker, humorist Will Rogers, actress-comedian Lucille Ball, actor Johnny Depp, hairstylist Vidal Sasoon, entertainer Lawrence Welk, actor Sean Connery, country singer Glen Campbell, baseball manager Casey Stengel, author Louis L'Amour, comedian Red Skelton, actor Jackie Gleason, inventor George Eastman (Kodak camera), the "singing cowboy" Gene Autry, actress Demi Moore, entertainer Frank Sinatra, baseball player-manager Yogi Berra, actress-singer Julie Andrews

Answer: They are all high school (or elementary school!) dropouts.

A Detour to Success

Broadway mastermind George Gershwin dropped out of high school at age fifteen. His achievements include *Rhapsody in Blue*, *Porgy and Bess*, and *An American in Paris*.

Leading man Pierce Brosnan dropped out of high school and ran away with the circus, working as a fire eater.

Songwriter Bernie Taupin, creator of "Candle in the Wind," "Bennie and the Jets," and "Goodbye Yellow Brick Road," dropped out of high school at age fifteen.

Ray Kroc, founder of the McDonald's franchise, is a high school dropout. He started out by selling paper cups to earn a living.

Comedian, actress, and talk-show co-host Whoopi Goldberg worked in a funeral parlor after dropping out of high school. She was also a welfare recipient.

Robert DeNiro dropped out of school at the age of 13 and joined a street gang.

Heavyweight boxing champion George Foreman, winner of the Olympic gold medal, dropped out of high school his freshman year and joined a gang, participating in robbery and battery.

Law and Order

Comedian Tim Allen, star of the hit sitcom *Home Improvement*, spent nearly three years in a federal penitentiary in the early 1970s for dealing drugs.

Civil rights leader and humanitarian activist Malcom X served a ten-year prison sentence for burglary before turning his life around and becoming a minister.

Literary genius Dante wrote the *Divine Comedy* under a sentence of death during twenty years in exile.

Musician/superstar Jimi Hendrix was convicted of car theft and sentenced to two years in prison. He was also given the option of enlisting in the army instead. He chose the army but was thrown out for bad behavior.

Actor Nick Nolte was convicted of counterfeiting in 1962 and served an extended probation.

Rock 'n Roll Hall of Fame legend Chuck Berry was convicted of armed robbery and served a three-year sentence.

Academy Award nominee Ryan O'Neal was jailed for two months for an assault and battery conviction in his younger years.

Sir Walter Raleigh wrote the *History of the World* during a thirteen year imprisonment.

109. Have patience with all things, but chiefly have patience with yourself. Do not lose courage in considering your own imperfections, but instantly set about remedying them. Every day begin the task anew.

ST. FRANCIS DE SALES

Today is a new day. You will get out of it just what you put into it. If you have made mistakes, no matter how significant, there is always another chance for you. Even if you have tried and failed again and again, you may have a fresh start any moment you choose, for this thing that we call "failure" is not the falling down, but the staying down.

MARY PICKFORD

110. With every rising of the sun, think of your life as just begun.

ANONYMOUS

Each day is a little life, every waking and rising a little birth.

ARTHUR SCHOPENHAUER

111. Choose to believe that failure is an event, never a person.

WILLIAM D. BROWN

I've never met a person, I don't care what his condition, in whom I could not see possibilities. I don't care how much a man may consider himself a failure, I believe in him, for he can change the thing that is wrong in his life anytime he is prepared and ready to do so. Whenever he develops the desire, he can take away from his life the thing that is defeating it. The capacity for reformation and change lies within all of us. We simply must choose it.

PRESTON BRADLEY

112. See the world made new every morning, as if it were the morning of the first day. Then, make the most of it.

JOHN FINLEY

Each golden sunrise ushers in new opportunities for those who retain faith in themselves and keep their chins up. Meet each sunrise with confidence. Fill every golden minute with right thinking and worthwhile endeavor. Do this and there will be joy for you in each golden sunset.

ALONZO BENN

High Hurdles

O. Henry, the famed American author of hundreds of short stories including *The Gift of the Magi*, was jailed for three years for fleeing the U.S. on embezzlement charges before writing his greatest works.

CNN talk show host Larry King was arrested in 1971 on grand larceny charges and was subsequently fired from radio station WIOD, Channel 4 television, and the *Sun Reporter* newspaper as a result of being entangled in the investigation. The case was never settled because the statute of limitations ran out. King went on to become a broadcasting legend despite his legal difficulties in early life.

Country Music Hall of Fame singer/songwriter Merle Haggard, who recorded thirty-eight #1 hits during his career, turned twenty-one years old in San Quentin Prison. Haggard later wrote his hit song "Mama Tried" about the experience of that birthday. Little Merle began getting into trouble with petty crimes as a nine-year-old, and it didn't take long before he was a teenager and arrested for shoplifting, truancy, petty larceny, assault, attempted burglary, and a subsequent successful robbery of a Bakersfield, California tavern. He was sent to prison where he didn't behave much better, running a gambling and brewing racket from his cell. Haggard's life turned around in prison after he attended three of Johnny Cash's concerts at San Quentin. Seeing Cash perform inspired Haggard to straighten up and pursue his love of music. Several years later, at another Cash concert, Haggard came up to Johnny and told him, "I certainly enjoyed your show at San Quentin." Cash responded, "Merle, I don't remember you being in that show," to which Merle replied, "I wasn't in that show, Johnny, I was in that audience."

113. Don't fret over what you'd do with your life if you could live it over. Get busy with what you have left. Begin anew!

ANONYMOUS

Onward and upward!

KATHARINE WHITE

114. Realize that you will encounter defeats, but you must never be defeated, ever!

MAYA ANGELOU

Stand up! What are you doing down on your face?

JOSHUA 7:10

Always remember that it is never too late in fiction or in real life to revise.

NANCY THAYER

He Dared to Dream

Have I not commanded you? Be strong and courageous. Do not be terrified; do not be discouraged.

JOSHUA 1:9

Ben Carson was born in Detroit, Michigan, in 1951, and he and his brother were raised by their mother, who often worked two or three jobs to support the family.

As a young boy, Ben didn't like to read books, and he was always at the bottom of his class. He still remembers how in the fifth grade he was failing almost every subject, but he remembers one incident in particular.

His class had just taken a math quiz, and it was the custom for the students to report their math scores out loud, so the teacher could record the scores in her book.

When he got his quiz back from the girl behind him who had corrected it, he had gotten zero out of thirty right.

He tried to mumble "none," hoping the teacher would misunderstand him, and she did. She thought he had said "nine," and she raved about how wonderful that was until the girl behind him couldn't stand it any longer, and she corrected the teacher.

Everybody roared with laughter, and Ben was so humiliated that he just wanted to evaporate into thin air and disappear forever.

It was about this time when he heard about mission doctors who helped people in far-off lands, but his mother reminded him that he could never be a doctor if he didn't start reading books and stop watching so much TV.

From then on, every time he reached for the TV, his mother told him to read a book instead. She also insisted that he and his brother write book reports for the books they read. They didn't know at the time that their mother couldn't read their reports because of her third-grade education. The more he read, the more interesting books became, and before long he was devouring them. Within two years he rose from the bottom of his class to the top.

But his problems weren't over yet. He also had a pathological temper, which scared his family. He remembers one time when he tried to hit his mother in the head with a hammer because he didn't want to wear something she wanted him to wear.

He also put a three-inch gash in a classmate's forehead with his lock when he tried to close Ben's locker.

And then at fourteen, he stabbed a friend in the abdomen with a large camping knife when his friend tried to change the radio station they were listening to. Fortunately, the knife hit his friends' belt buckle, which saved his life, but this shook Ben up so badly that he went home, locked himself in the bathroom, and did some serious thinking.

He knew that in spite of the good grades he was now earning, he could end up in jail, reform school, or the grave because of his temper and never be the doctor he wanted to be.

He spent three hours in the bathroom praying about his temper and reading from the Book of Proverbs in his Bible. When he came out of the bathroom, his temper was gone. He had concluded during his stint in the bathroom that if people can make you angry, they can control you, and he refused to give that control to anyone else.

During his last year of high school, he had to choose a college, but each college application cost ten dollars. He had only a single ten-dollar bill, which meant he could apply to only one school, so he chose Yale University after watching the Yale team beat Harvard on his favorite TV quiz show, *College Bowl*.

Fortunately, he was accepted by Yale and received an academic scholarship that covered most of his college expenses.

He worked hard at Yale and read even more than his teacher assigned. After Yale, he attended the Michigan Medical School, where he discovered his surgical skills. Again, he would put a knife in his hand, but this time to save lives, not to take them.

During his hospital training, he discovered his love of neurosurgery, which, along with his natural ability, would soon take him to the top of his field.

When he was ready to begin his internship, he applied to Johns Hopkins Hospital, which received over 125 applications to join its neurosurgery division each year, and it accepted only two. These odds did not scare him off because he recalled his mother's words that he could become whatever he wanted to be.

He was accepted at Johns Hopkins and always treated everyone with equal respect, whether an orderly or another doctor. He also learned to deal with racism when some of the nurses would assume he was an orderly because he was black or when some of the patients would not allow him to touch them because he was black.

At age thirty-three he became the director of pediatric neurosurgery at Johns Hopkins, the youngest chief of pediatric neurosurgery in United States history, and he began to see some very important cases.

One of these cases was a four-year-old girl with a severe form of epilepsy that sometimes caused her to have as many as a hundred seizures a day. Ben and his medical team performed a dangerous operation where they removed part of the left side of her brain (hemispherectomy). If the surgery was successful, she would be free of her seizures. But if the surgery failed, she could die. The surgery was successful, and now the whole medical world was watching Dr. Ben Carson to see what he would do next.

He was also the primary surgeon in the dramatic and successful twenty-two-hour operation in 1987 that separated the West German Siamese twins who were joined at the back of the head.

Ben attained his personal dream of becoming a doctor and conquered his own personal demons of anger and insecurity while doing so.

Children are very important to him, and he spends time today speaking to schools and community centers—encouraging young people to work hard and believe in themselves and not let others set limits for them.

SANDRA McLEOD HUMPHREY

Strong in the Broken Places

In April 1968, U.S. army Captain Max Cleland had one month left on his tour of duty in Vietnam. Jumping out of a helicopter, he stooped to pick up a grenade he thought had fallen off his belt. It exploded. The blast jammed his eyeballs back into his skull, blinding him.

When he could see again, he realized his right hand was gone. So, too, his right leg and knee. He would have screamed but he couldn't—a piece of shrapnel had cut his esophagus. After five hours of battlefield surgery and forty-one pints of blood, he survived. Months later at the Walter Reed Army Hospital, he wished he hadn't. He descended into despair. He drank heavily. Hospitalized for the flu, he hit rock bottom on Easter Sunday, 1969. He sank into a very deep depression, sobbing uncontrollably, bitter over the past, and afraid of the future. The present seemed unbearable. He had to choose, live or die, and right at that moment he chose life.

He decided to fight back and make it through his rehab. How? Inspiration, celebration, and challenge. He says he was inspired by the tenacity of George Washington, Winston Churchill, FDR, and Jesus. He would repeat Churchill's words to himself: "Never give in. Never. Never. Never. Never." He also celebrated each victory, no matter how small. He pushed to have his doctors outfit him with artificial limbs and eventually he walked.

Then he pushed himself in new ways. He ran for a seat in the Georgia legislature in 1970 and won. He was appointed head of the Veterans Administration in 1976 and elected to the U.S. Senate in 1996. He had been to hell and come all the way back again. Today his life stands as a testimony to what he believes: "We think adversity itself is darkness, but the reality of the darkness is that it can serve to illuminate the light."

JOHN A. SARKETT

115. Don't dwell on your misfortunes from the past. The longer you dwell on them, the greater will be their power to harm you.

VOLTAIRE

The past cannot be changed. The future is yet in your power.

HUGH WHITE

40
NE
20
360
N
340
320
NW
300
120
SE
140
160
S
180
200
SW

Progressing Forward

"The greatest thing in the world is not so much where we stand, but in which direction we are moving."

OLIVER WENDELL HOLMES

116. Understand that progress involves risk; you can't steal second base and keep your foot on first.

FREDERICK WILCOX

The important thing is this: to be able at any moment to sacrifice what you are for what you could become.

CHARLES DU BOS

117. Realize that if you don't risk anything, you risk even more.

ERICA JONG

Be careful about being too careful.

BERYL PFIZER

Be not afraid of going slowly.
Be afraid only of standing still.

CHINESE PROVERB

118. Remember that modest beginnings can produce significant results.

COUNT ISTVAN SZECHENY

Hollywood leading man Brad Pitt started out on the bottom rung of the ladder like everyone else. His first "acting" job was to dress up as a chicken and attract customers to a restaurant near his home.

119. Don't wait for inspiration. You have to go after it with a club.

JACK LONDON

Passion is the key ingredient for achieving success—passion about who you are, who you are tying to become, and where you are going.

DONALD TRUMP

120. If your ship doesn't come in, swim out to it.

JONATHAN WINTERS

I would go into a place and say, "I'm a comedian," and they'd say, "Get out of here." Then I'd put a $50 bill on the bar. I'd say, "Just let me tell some jokes, and if people leave or I embarrass the customers, you keep the fifty bucks." The wager always worked.

JAY LENO

121. When opportunity knocks, open the door even if you're in your bathrobe.

HEATHER ZSCHOCK

If you hold back on life, life holds back on you.

MARY MORRISSEY

A Fighting Spirit

Make no small plans. They have no power to stir the soul.

NICCOLO MACHIAVELLI

Sylvester Stallone struggled to build momentum when he began to pursue his dream of becoming an actor because of his slurred speech, droopy lower lip, and crooked left eye. (All of these were the result of a facial nerve which was severed by forceps when he was born.)

Stallone faced multiple rejections at acting interviews and remembers: "I was thrown out of more than 1,500 offices in New York. There aren't 1,500 agents in New York, but I was thrown out of some offices six, seven, eight, and nine times. I was told to 'do something else' because nobody was going to listen to someone who 'looks dopey' and talks out of the side of his mouth."

Stallone's first acting job came as a result of being turned down for a job, but refusing to leave. When the manager returned the next morning and saw the desperate man still sitting in the chair, he hired him for a small part.

Stallone started writing screenplays, receiving similar rejections, and it wasn't long before he ran out of money and could barely feed himself. He would regularly wander into a nearby library to keep warm during the colder months when he couldn't pay his heat bill.

One day Stallone watched a boxing match between Weppner and Ali. Weppner, the underdog, was getting slaughtered, but kept holding his ground and coming back for more, fighting with everything in him. Stallone was inspired. He began to write a screenplay based on the inspiration he felt from watching Weppner try to win despite impossible odds. He wrote for three days straight and completed the entire script to *Rocky*. When he tried to sell the script, however, he received more rejections.

He was so poor by this time that he decided to sell his "best friend," his dog. Stallone waited outside a local liquor store and asked people if they would buy his dog for $50. He ended up selling his dog to a man who haggled him down to $25. "I walked away and cried," said Stallone.

Eventually two executives read the screenplay and loved it, but when Stallone told them that he wanted to play the part of Rocky, they declined. They told him that he was a writer, not an actor, and they wanted a well-known actor, Burt Reynolds or Ryan O'Neill. Stallone refused their offer of $125,000, despite his poverty. (Remember, he was starving!)

A couple of weeks later they offered him $250,000 if he *not* play Rocky. Again Stallone declined: "It's *my* script, and *I'm* Rocky."

The offer rose to $325,000. Stallone went home and looked at the balance in his checking account—his entire net worth—and saw it was $100. He picked up the phone and responded to their offer by saying, "No."

Eventually they agreed to allow Stallone to play Rocky, but lowered their price to $35,000 because they thought the movie would fail. The first thing Stallone did when he received the money was to go back to the liquor store and buy his dog back. He waited for three days for the guy to come by and offered him $50, but the man refused. The offer kept rising—$100, $500, $1,000—but the man wouldn't budge. Stallone ended up giving him $15,000 and a part in the movie. The fellow (and the dog) are both in *Rocky*.

Of course we all know what happened with *Rocky*. It was a box office smash and nominated for ten Academy Awards including Best Actor and Best Original Screen Play.

Endless Human Potential

122. Remember that your dream and passion to succeed must be stronger than your fear of failure.

TERRI BOWERSOCK

Think of fear like alcohol. It impairs judgment. Never make any decisions while under its influence.

GREGORY BERNS

123. Avoid procrastination. When there's a hill to climb, don't think that waiting will make it smaller.

H. JACKSON BROWN

Hesitation enhances fear.

NIGERIAN PROVERB

124. You can get there from here. You can. Walk through the fear.

MARY ANNE RADMACHER-HERSHEY

Many of our fears are tissuepaper-thin, and a single courageous step would carry us clear through them.

BRENDAN FRANCIS

125. Never forget that doubting your ability to get what you long for is like trying to reach east by traveling west.

CHARLES BAUDOUIN

Our doubts are traitors.

WILLIAM SHAKESPEARE

126. Remember that many a man has walked up to the opportunity for which he has long been preparing himself, looked it full in the face, and then begun to get cold feet.

B. C. FORBES

Our chief defect is that we are more given to talking about things than we are to doing them.

JAWAHARLAL NEHRU

127. Understand that you must expect things of yourself before you can do them.

MICHAEL JORDAN

Achievement is more of a function of the mind than it is of the muscle.

JOHN SARKETT

What I admire most in Columbus is not his having discovered a world, but having gone out in search of it on the faith of an opinion.

ANNE JACQUES TURGOT

Our business in life is not to get ahead of others but to get ahead of ourselves—to break our own records, to outstrip our yesterdays by our today.

STEWARD B. JOHNSON

Odd Jobs of the Rich and Famous

It is by tiny steps we ascend the stars.

JACK LEEDSTROM

Singer Davy Jones of The Monkees was a horse jockey.

Rock 'n roll legend Little Richard sold snake oil at carnivals.

Hollywood heartthrob Robert Redford drove a forklift at a Standard Oil refinery. He was fired.

Top-selling record artist Willie Nelson, who recorded the hit song, "Mamas, Don't Let Your Babies Grow Up to Be Cowboys," was a pig farmer.

Academy Award winning actor Dustin Hoffman worked as a janitor; so did singer Mariah Carey.

Actor Burt Lancaster was a refrigerator repairman.

Screen legend Yul Brynner, who played starring roles in *The Ten Commandments* and *The King and I*, took a job as a trapeze artist in a Paris circus.

Humphrey Bogart, one of the most recognized stars of the twentieth century, earned money to pay his living expenses by playing chess for 50 cents a game.

Sex symbol and singing sensation Madonna worked in a doughnut shop. Her husband, movie director Guy Ritchie, dug sewers. He was also a furniture mover, until he was fired.

Aristotle Onassis, who gained worldwide fame in the shipping industry, and later became one of history's wealthiest men, worked as a telephone operator.

Actor Clark Gable, best known for his role in *Gone With the Wind*, was a lumberjack.

Feature-film leading man Bruce Willis worked as a security guard at a nuclear power plant.

Actress Goldie Hawn was a go-go dancer, and so was singer-actress Bette Midler.

Actor-musician Desi Arnaz, co-star of the *I Love Lucy* show and husband to Lucille Ball, cleaned canary cages for a living after arriving in America from Cuba.

Musician Axl Rose, of Guns N' Roses, participated in a scientific study to earn money to pay his bills. He received $8.00 an hour to sit and smoke cigarettes.

Singing sensation David Bowie worked as a mime.

Sonny Bono, of the "Sonny and Cher" duo, went to work every day in an aircraft factory.

Actor Steve McQueen sold pencils.

Singer-songwriter Perry Como, who recorded more than a dozen #1 hits, initially failed in the music business. He quit and went back home to Pennsylvania where he worked as a barber.

Actor Tony Danza owned a car wash before making his entrance into Hollywood.

Comedian and talk show host Jon Stewart started out as a bartender.

Country music superstar Johnny Cash was a door-to-door salesman.

Broadway actress Colleen Dewhurst worked as an elevator operator.

128. When you come to the edge of all the light you know, and are about to step off into the darkness of the unknown, have faith. Believe that one of two things will happen: There will either be something solid for you to stand on or you will be taught how to fly.

BARBARA WINTER

It is only when I dally with what I am about, look back and aside, instead of keeping my eyes straight forward, that I feel these cold sinkings of the heart.

SIR WALTER SCOTT

129. Remember that destiny is not a matter of chance. It is a matter of choice.

WILLIAM JENNINGS BRYAN

I've always been in the right place at the right time. Of course, I steered myself there.

BOB HOPE

130. Understand that you will lose much by fearing to attempt.

J. N. MOFFIT

What really matters is what you do with what you have.

SHIRLEY LORD

Did you know?

Pablo Casals, the greatest cellist who ever lived, continued to practice faithfully for at least six hours daily even when he was nearly 100 years old. When he was asked why, he responded: "Because I think I'm making progress."

131. Never forget that big shots are only little shots who kept on shooting.

CHRISTOPHER MORLEY

You can have big plans, but it is the small choices that have the greatest power to draw us toward the future we want to create.

ROBERT COOPER

132. Make it a habit to do a little more each day than you think you possibly can.

LOWELL THOMAS

Success, real success, in any endeavor demands more from an individual than most people are willing to offer—not more than they are capable of offering.

JAMES ROCHE

Encouragement Gives a Lift

I stopped by Dairy Queen, purchased a sandwich, and sat down in the crowded dining room next to a family celebrating their son's basketball game over an ice-cream cake. Since the aisles were especially narrow, I soon felt like I was part of the party.

"So, your team must have won this afternoon," I commented.

The little fellow smiled and wholeheartedly announced, "No, we lost 24 to 2!"

"Well, you must have made the only basket then," I said.

"No," he responded, "I missed all of the eight shots I took, but three of them did hit the rim."

This child was elated. I was confused. *They were celebrating because his team lost the game and because he had missed eight baskets!?!?!?* Seldom am I at a loss for words, but the only response I could muster up at that moment was a blank stare (and a very large, insincere looking smile). I had absolutely no clue as to why this child was so happy.

After another mouthful of cake, and still grinning from ear-to-ear, he added, "We're having a party because last week I missed nine shots and none of them even came anywhere near to the backboard. Dad says that all of my practicing this week really paid off. I'm making progress."

ROCHELLE PENNINGTON

133. Practice patience. All great accomplishments require time.

DAVID JOSEPH SCHWARTZ

Dear God, I pray for patience…and I want it RIGHT NOW!!

OREN ARNOLD

134. Give consideration to the fact that victories are won not in miles, but in inches. Win a little now, hold your ground, and later win a little more.

LOUIS L'AMOUR

How can a society that exists on instant mashed potatoes, packaged cake mixes, and frozen dinners teach patience?

PAUL SWEENEY

Don't Quit

When things go wrong, as they sometimes will,
When the road you're trudging seems all uphill,
When the funds are low and the debts are high,
And you want to smile, but you have to sigh,
When care is pressing you down a bit,
Rest, if you must—but don't you quit.

Life is strange with its twists and turns,
As every one of us sometimes learns,
And many a failure turns about
When he might have won had he stuck it out.
Don't give up, though the pace seems slow—
You might succeed with another blow.

Success is failure turned inside out;
The silver tint of the clouds of doubt.
And you never can tell how close you are,
It may be near when it seems afar;
So stick to the fight when you're hardest hit—
It's when things seem worst that you mustn't quit.

EDGAR GUEST

135. Memorize this six-word formula for success: Think things through—then follow through.

EDWARD RICKENBACKER

Begin at the beginning, and go until you come to the end. Then stop.

LEWIS CARROLL

136. Understand that effort is a commitment to seeing a goal through to the end, not just until you get tired of it.

HOWARD CATO

There is genius in persistence. It conquers all opposers. It gives confidence. It annihilates obstacles. Everybody believes in a determined man. People know that when he undertakes a thing, the battle is half won, for his rule is to accomplish whatever he sets out to do.

ORISON SWETT MARDEN

No one would have crossed the ocean if he could have gotten off the ship in the middle of a storm.

CHARLES F. KETTERING

137. Beware. Your road to success will be dotted with many tempting parking places.

ANONYMOUS

You cannot advance when you concentrate on retreat.

SUE SIKKING

Did you know?

R. H. Macy, founder of the famous New York City store (and namesake of the Macy's Thanksgiving Day Parade), failed several times before he achieved mega-success in the retail industry.

Macy's first store, a dry-goods business in California, folded. His second store, another dry-goods store opened in Massachusetts, also failed. Macy then opened a store in New York City which was soon robbed. Then it burned to the ground. Macy, not to be "easily dissuaded," refused to give up. He re-built the store and finally succeeded.

138. Hold on; hold fast; hold out. Patience is genius.

GEORGE DE BUFFON

I realized early on that success was tied to not giving up. Most people in this business gave up and went on to other things. If you simply didn't give up, you would outlast the people who came in on the bus with you.

HARRISON FORD

139. Realize that the way to succeed is to never quit. That's it.

ALEX HAILEY

Endurance is one of the most difficult disciplines, but it is to the one who endures that the final victory comes.

BUDDHA

140. Expect occasional reverses and periodic failures. You must somehow get comfortable with the reality of these.

SAM COLLINS

All problems become smaller if you don't dodge them, but confront them instead. Touch a thistle timidly, and it pricks you; grasp it boldly, and its spine crumbles.

WILLIAM S. HALSEY

141. Don't worry about your difficulties. Change them. Worry is as useless as a handle on a snowball.

MITZI CHANDLER

You can think about your problems or you can worry about them, and there is a vast difference between the two. Worry is thinking that has turned toxic. It is the jarring music that goes round and round and never comes to either a climax or conclusion. Thinking works its way through problems to conclusions and decisions; worry leaves you in a state of tensely suspended animation. When you worry, you go over the same ground endlessly and come out the same place you started. Thinking makes progress from one place to another; worry remains static. The problem is to change worry into thinking—and anxiety into creative action.

HAROLD WALKER

H. J. Heinz and Company

Success isn't built on success. It is built on failure and frustration—sometimes catastrophic—and learning to turn it around.

SUMNER REDSTONE

Of all the stories of entrepreneurs who rose from bankruptcy to greatness, none is more inspiring than that of Henry John Heinz, founder of H. J. Heinz & Company. Heinz grew a two-acre horseradish garden into one of the worlds largest food packagers, with annual sales today totaling in the billions of dollars.

Born to a Pittsburgh brickmaker in 1844, Heinz developed a green thumb as a boy, tending the family's two-acre garden. The tastiest bounty of that tiny garden was horseradish, a plant that Heinz's ancestors grew for centuries in the river valleys of Kallstadt in Bavaria. Young Heinz harvested so much of the stuff that the family had him sell the extra quantities to neighbors. At Heinz's suggestion, the family pre-grated the horseradish root and sold it at a premium. The Heinzes innovated further by selling the grated horseradish in clear bottles so people could see what they were buying. At age 16, Heinz had four employees bottling three acres worth of horseradish. In 1869, he was selling enough horseradish to buy an office in Chicago as well as a team of horse and wagons.

Things turned sour for Heinz when he expanded into the pickle business. In 1875, he entered into a contract with an Illinois farmer promising to buy all the cucumbers he grew for 60 cents a bushel. Beating 50-to-1 odds, the cucumber crop hit unheard of levels. Heinz took delivery of so many cucumbers that they blocked the entrance to his office. At the same time a financial panic swept the nation, shutting off credit and drying up sales. In 1875, Heinz was forced into bankruptcy. Evicted from his office and bereft of staff or supplies, Heinz almost despaired. He wrote in his diary: "No Christmas gifts to exchange. Sally seemed grieved, and cried…I wish no one such trials." Another entry sadly records: "Bought a cheap $16 horse…. He is blind."

Heinz made his comeback by borrowing from his brothers and sisters who scraped together $3,000 in capital. Soon Heinz began selling a product that would keep him out of the red for good—tomato ketchup.

ROLAND GARY JONES

142. Understand that the difference between getting somewhere and nowhere is the courage to make a start.

CHARLES SCHWAB

In the long run, men hit only what they aim at.

HENRY DAVID THOREAU

143. Be determined. You can have anything you want if you want it desperately enough. You must want it with an exuberance that erupts through the skin and joins with the energy that created the world.

SHEILA GRAHAM

Few people during their lifetime come anywhere near exhausting the resources dwelling within them.

ADMIRAL RICHARD BYRD

Pursue Excellence

Good, better, best.
Never rest
Until good is better
And better best.

MOTHER GOOSE

144. Make up your mind at the very outset that your work is going to stand for quality; that you are going to stamp a superiority upon everything that goes out of your hands; that whatever you do shall bear the hallmark of excellence.

ORISON SWETT MARDEN

Whatever is worth doing, is worth doing well.

EARL OF CHESTERFIELD

145. Give to the world the best you have and the best will come back to you.

MADELINE BRIDGES

When you consider that Shakespeare produced his great works, thousands and thousands of pages, writing with a bird's tail feather, you realize that it isn't always what you have to work with that matters, but how you work with what you have.

RICHARD FERNANDEZ

I am seeking, I am striving, I am in it with all of my heart.

VINCENT VAN GOGH

Attention to Detail

Always live up to your full potential in every endeavor.

JOE ROBBIE

In front of the Grenoble Museum's most prized painting was a little old man. In his hand was a brush. On his arm was a box of oil colors. A museum attendant, making his rounds, came upon the old fellow just as he was starting to repaint a corner of the canvas—a famous Bonnard painting. With a howl of anger, the attendant pounced, and the timid little man, splattering protest, was hauled off to the local police department. The officers there were posed with an interesting problem for the so-called vandal was the painter Bonnard himself. Bonnard, who had a habit of never being really satisfied with his canvases, would try to touch them up whenever he could get near them.

BITS AND PIECES

146. Hold yourself responsible for a higher standard than anyone else expects of you.

HENRY WARD BEECHER

I discovered at an early age that the biggest difference between average people and great people can be explained in three little words—"and then some." Top people do what is expected of them, and then some. They are considerate and thoughtful of others, and then some. They meet their responsibilities fairly and squarely, and then some. They can be counted on in any situation, and then some.

JAMES E. BYRNES

147. Go the extra yard. It makes a mile of difference.

ANONYMOUS

Whatever your hand finds to do, do it with all of your might.

ECCLESIASTES 9:10

Man Enough for the Job

No duty is too small for great men.

ANONYMOUS

An incident is told of the first American war about an officer who set his men to cutting some trees down which were needed to make a bridge.

There were not nearly enough men, and work was getting on very slowly.

Up rode a commanding-looking man who spoke to the officer in charge. The officer was urging on his men but was doing nothing himself.

"You haven't enough men for the job, have you?" asked the gentleman who rode up on horseback.

"No, sir. We need some help."

"Why don't you lend a hand yourself?" asked the man on horseback.

"Me, sir? Why, I am a corporal," replied the officer, looking rather affronted at the mere suggestion.

"Ah, true," quietly replied the other, and getting off his horse he labored with the men until the job was done. Then he mounted again, and as he rode off he said to the officer, "Corporal, the next time you have a job to put through and too few men to do it you had better send for the Commander-in-Chief, and I will come again."

It was General George Washington.

ELLA LYMAN CABOT

The real contest is always between what you've done and what you are capable of doing. You measure yourself against yourself and nobody else.

GEOFFREY GABERINO

From Tears to Cheers

No life ever grows great until it is focused, dedicated, and disciplined.

HARRY EMERSON FOSDICK

It has been my experience that one stumbles across life's most profound lessons in the most unexpected places—places like a neighborhood Little League baseball diamond.

Our son's first game of the season was scheduled for an evening in early May on a league that included grades six through eight. While some boys were third-year veterans on the team, our little guy, a sixth grader, was among the new recruits.

The usual crowd of parents had gathered as I took my seat on a weather-eaten plank third row from the top. Sandwiched between a cotton candy-faced youngster and somebody's mother, I checked the scoreboard. Fourth inning already. As my attention moved from the scoreboard, I glanced at the pitchers mound. Jason Voldner?

Jason was undoubtedly the most well-liked and good-natured boy on the team, but athletically, his participation had been limited to the alternating positions of far right field or bench—the latter, unfortunately, more frequently. Having spent an uncountable number of hours as a spectator (on an equally uncountable number of varying bleachers), it is my belief that every ballfield has its own version of Jason Voldner—without exception.

The Jasons of the world show up at a tender young age for their first Saturday morning T-ball practice, oiled glove in hand, but by the end of this long awaited "chance to play ball," the heavy-hearted Jasons return home remembering the boy who hit further, the boy who ran faster, and the boy who actually knew what he was supposed to do with the glove.

And ability is not only recognized, it's utilized, allowing for the exceptional players to become even more so, while the Jasons wait their turn to play the seventh inning. Right field. Their allotted playing time is not only limited, it's conditional—only if the team is already winning. If not, the Jasons have simply been waiting to go home. And eventually they stay there.

Yet here was Jason Voldner pitching what I would say to be the game of his lifetime (had there been anything to compare it to).

Turning to comment to anyone willing to listen, I now recognized the "somebody's mother" beside me as belonging to Jason. "Such talent," I offered. "I've never seen your son pitch before." In a voice of quiet resolve she responded, "Neither have I." Then she continued with a story.

Four weeks ago, she had chauffeured a car full of boys, her son included, to this same baseball diamond for their first spring practice. Just before dusk, the next carpool mother dropped Jason off after practice. As the van pulled up, Jason emerged from behind the sliding door.

"His face was a combination of dirt smudges and rain streaks, and would have masked from anyone but me that he was upset," she said. "My immediate concern was for an injury, but there was none."

Probing questions led her no closer to the elusive pain. By bedtime, she knew no more that she did back on the curb. This would change shortly.

She continued, "Sometime in the hours that followed, I was awakened by choking sobs—Jason's. At his bedside, broken words were telling his story. "Waiting. Eighth grade. Sick of right field. Eighth grade."

As Jason's mother calmed her son, he further explained that Matthew, a sixth-grader, was going to play second base "because his dad is coaching"; John, a sixth-grader, was assigned to shortstop "because he's Matthew's friend"; and Brian, yet another sixth-grader, was the new catcher "because his brother is on the team."

(I wondered where her story was going and began to squirm uncomfortably knowing that every one of the boys she just named had parents within earshot of our conversation.)

Jason continued crying, "Not fair. Not fair. Not fair." Listening to Jason, his mother's heart ached for him.

There should be a word that takes empathy to another level; a word for the exclusive use of parents.

"While Jason was waiting for me to agree with him," said his mother, "I was making the difficult decision not to. One has to be careful when having a direct and lasting effect on another person's negative emotions. Often times, agreement may appear to be the most caring and loyal means of help, but in reality, it can actually work to the contrary as you reinforce the negative feelings."

"So, first I explained to Jason that until we were ready to assist the coach with his responsibilities, we would trust his judgments as worthy. Secondly, I reminded him how seldom we passed the vacant lot on the corner of our block without finding the three sixth-graders in question involved in a random, unscheduled game of ball. Playing infield is not about being in the sixth grade or in the eighth I told him; it's about working hard and practicing your abilities. It's not about preferential treatment. I then asked him if his teacher gives him an 'A' just for showing up or if the workers at his dad's job get promoted 'just because.' I explained that all through life, we come into contact with individuals possessing a focused ambition for what they are pursuing—on the ball field, in the classroom, in the workplace. Some even possess natural talent."

"Does this mean you are unable to achieve what they have? Certainly not. You simply have to choose to work harder. Resentment, blame, and excuses will only poison your potential."

Jason's mother then tucked her son back into bed with these words: "You're disappointed that the coach doesn't believe in you, Jason, but before you can expect others to believe in you, you have to believe in yourself. The coach is basing his placements on the performances he has seen thus far. If you truly feel you deserve a position other than right field, then prove it." With those words she kissed him goodnight.

She smiled as she watched the next pitch, and added, "We spoke more in

Did you know?

Michelangelo endured seven long years of lying on his back on top of scaffolding to paint the ceiling of the Sistine Chapel, considered his greatest work. He became so entranced in his painting that he forgot to eat many times, and could even be found sleeping on the scaffolding instead of going to bed.

those few minutes that night than we have in the past few weeks since it seems. Our contact recently has been through notes written by Jason and left behind on the kitchen table: "Gone to practice. Gone to prove it."

She paused and then added, "And he did."

Yes, it has been my experience that one stumbles across life's most profound lessons in the most unexpected places—like a neighborhood Little League baseball diamond, while sitting on a weather-eaten plank third row from the top.

ROCHELLE PENNINGTON

148. Compete with yourself. Set your teeth and dive into the job of breaking your own record.

PAPYRUS

Every day you must try to make yourself grow. This you can do.

MAXWELL MALTZ

149. When you are not practicing, remember that someone somewhere is practicing, and when you meet him he will win.

ED MACAULEY

Alexander Graham Bell, inventor of the telephone, filed his patent only a few hours before Elisha Gray filed her patent. Ms. Gray was another inventor who was working on a similar telephone device at the exact same time.

150. Accept nothing nearly right or "good enough."

HENRY ROYCE

Average is your enemy.

PEARCE "ROCKY" LANE

151. Ask yourself: "If I don't have time to do it right, when will I have time to do it over?"

ANONYMOUS

It takes less time to do a thing right than it does to explain why you did it wrong.

HENRY WADSWORTH LONGFELLOW

152. Do each daily task to the fullest of your ability. Act as though the eye of opportunity was always upon you.

WILLIAM FEATHER

No one ever attains eminent success by simply doing what is required of him; it is the amount of excellence over and above the required that determines the greatness and ultimate distinction.

CHARLES ADAMS

Did you know?

Cesar Ritz, founder of the grandest hotel in Paris, refused to open his establishment in 1898 until he had personally slept one night in every single room in order to test the comfort and quality his guests would experience.

Doing your best at this moment puts you in the best place for the next moment.

OPRAH WINFREY

Improvising Under Pressure

Nicolo Paganini was a well-known and gifted nineteenth-century violinist. His most memorable concert, however, was one marked by unexpected challenges rather than easy success. The concert was performed with a full orchestra before a packed house in Italy. Those who heard him play say that Paganini's technique was incredible, and his tone fantastic. Toward the end of the concert, Paganini was astounding his rapt audience with a very difficult composition when one string on his violin suddenly snapped and hung limply from his instrument. Paganini frowned only briefly, shook his head, and continued to play, improvising beautifully.

Then to everyone's surprise, including Paganini's, a second string broke. Shortly thereafter, a third string snapped. It seemed like a slapstick comedy routine as Paganini stood before the awed crowd with strings dangling from his Stradivarius violin. Instead of leaving the stage to repair his instrument, he stood firm. He calmly completed the difficult number on the one remaining string—a performance that won him applause, admiration, and enduring fame.

GOD'S LITTLE DAILY DEVOTIONAL

A Herculean Effort

Spectacular achievement is always preceded by spectacular preparation.

ROBERT SCHULLER

It's impossible. A quadriplegic in a wheelchair, competing in marathons, triathlons, and even in the famously grueling Ironman race. It's impossible, and yet here he comes again, across the finish line, ahead of half the others in the race, with that radiant smile spectators have come to expect and love.

Rick Hoyt has crossed over 631 of those finish lines in the last twenty years, often in the top fifty percent, sometimes even as the winner. But he never crosses alone. Sometimes in front of him, sometimes behind, is the other half of the Hoyt team, his father, Dick.

People say what Dick does is impossible too—a middle-aged man jogging mile after mile, pushing another man in a wheelchair. Peddling Rick on a bicycle up and down unforgiving hills. Pulling Rick two miles or more through the water as he swims.

But the Hoyt family has made a habit of doing the impossible.

When Rick was born in 1962, the doctors told his parents, Dick and Judy, that their newborn son would bring them nothing but heartache and urged them to put him in an institution. As a spastic quadriplegic with cerebral palsy, Rick would live out his life as a vegetable. That's what the doctors said. Never, the doctors warned, could their son be mainstreamed into society.

The Hoyts ignored the experts' advice and brought their son to their home in North Reading, Massachusetts. Dick and Judy were determined to raise him just like they would any other child. Back then, experts didn't know a lot about cerebral palsy and weren't sure of the full extent of Rick's disability. Learning to live with a child with severe disabilities was considered beyond the capabilities of almost any parent. But the Hoyts weren't typical parents. They set out to prove that "disabilities" are merely challenges meant to be overcome, not impassable barriers.

Rick's only way to communicate was by nodding his head yes or shaking it no. Speech professionals said he would never be able to speak. The Hoyts believed otherwise and raised $5,000 that they donated to Tufts University to help build the first interactive communicator. The device allowed a speechless person to "talk" by scrolling electronically through rows of letters and numbers and making selections to form complete messages. When Rick was twelve, the communicator was finally ready for testing. The engineers from Tufts and the entire Hoyt family excitedly stood around Rick, waiting to hear his very first words. Rick used his head to touch an electronic switch, spelling out "Go Bruins!"

"We all laughed," said Dick, "because he confirmed what we had believed all along—Rick had a healthy, active mind—and a sense of humor."

Because of Rick's revealed interest in sports, the entire family took him fishing, canoeing, and even rock climbing, strapping him to his father's back. The family witnessed Rick's sense of adventure and challenge and saw a person with a normal mind, human needs, and hopes who longed to be respected. The interactive communicator played a key role in enabling Rick to express himself and his interests and revealed his curious, intelligent personality. Yet schools refused to enroll Rick since he could not walk, feed himself, or talk on his own. At fourteen, because of his increasing ability to "speak" through his communicator and a new law mandating the right of all children to attend school, Rick finally gained admittance to high school, where special aides helped him with physical tasks he was unable to handle himself. It was during this remarkable period of personal growth that Rick found the catalyst for his incredible athletic career.

In 1977, when Rick was sixteen, he learned of a five-mile road race that would be held to benefit a college student who was injured in an automobile accident. Using his communicator, Rick told his dad that he wanted to "run" in the race as his contribution. Dick's initial reaction was shock. "I thought, I'm forty, a guy who jogs a couple of days a week to keep my weight down, but hardly a seasoned runner. I was concerned about how I could participate in such a race while pushing Rick in his wheelchair. But I knew it meant a lot to my son so I said, 'Okay we'll try it.'"

After the race, Dick could hardly move for two weeks. He was in agony. But one night as he soaked his aching muscles in Epsom salts, Rick came home and typed a message that changed Dick's life forever. It read: "Dad, when I'm running, it feels like I'm not handicapped anymore." Finally Rick had found something that gave him freedom like nothing else. At that point, Dick knew what he had to do. If Rick wanted to become an athlete and compete, Dick would loan him his arms and legs to make it happen. But to do so, Dick needed to design a lighter running chair so he wouldn't kill himself in the process.

Over the next two years, while Dick and an engineer designed and built the special chair, Rick and his father continued training and racing locally using the old chair. When the new chair was ready in September 1979, father and son entered their first official race, a five-mile race in Springfield, Massachusetts. They finished 150th out of 300 runners. They ran races in different cities every weekend. One of those races was the world-famous Boston Marathon—a grueling 26.2 miles. Rick and his father applied in the wheelchair division, where paraplegics had been racing on their own for years, but they were turned down because Rick, a quadriplegic, required a racing partner. Although the Hoyts were refused entrance into the race, they showed up anyway, lining up behind the wheelchairs. Neither the sponsors nor the organizing committee would even acknowledge their presence, but the spectators along the city streets sure did! They applauded and cheered them on every step of the way. When the Hoyts finished, the crowd was jubilant. Out of 7,400 runners, the Hoyts finished in the top 90 percent. The race was the first of many Boston Marathons they would enter and finish.

During these years, Rick also proved himself to be much more than just an unusual athlete. He earned a degree in special education from Boston University, becoming the first "nonspeaking" quadriplegic to graduate from college.

By 1984, Dick had become an accomplished runner and was invited to race in triathlons. (Triathlons are the Herculean races that combine long-distance swimming, long-distance bicycling, and cross-country running.) The organizers wanted Dick—but only if he would compete alone. He refused. The next year the organizers made the same offer, but again Dick refused to participate without his son. Dick told the organizers, "Rick was the one who got me into this, and I have no desire to compete without him. He is the one who drives me. Besides, without Rick, I wouldn't even know what to do with my arms."

Finally, the race officials approved Rick's participation if Dick could devise safe, durable equipment that would enable both of them to compete. Never mind that Dick didn't even know how to swim and hadn't been on a bicycle since he was six years old. After what his son had already accomplished, those seemed like small details to overcome.

Dick started training and devising the equipment that would help him tow Rick through water and pedal him by bicycle. The bicycle weighed 60 pounds,

Rick weighed 90, and Dick weighed 170—that would be 320 pounds moving up and down hills, pushing relentlessly across agonizing physical and mental barriers. Rick and Dick completed that triathlon and every subsequent triathlon they entered, usually finishing in the top half of the competition.

Along the way, Dick developed a motto: "There is nothing we cannot do together." Dick was right. Together, father and son completed the infamous Ironman competition, a race most people are happy just to survive—2.4 miles of swimming, 112 miles on a bike, and 26.2 miles of running. Because of the extreme conditions of the Ironman race located on the big island of Hawaii—100-degree heat, high humidity, and unrelenting hills—this race required special preparation. To train, they competed in local races every weekend for a year. During the week while Rick was in school, Dick trained alone daily. He swam up to two miles, ran eight miles and biked thirty-five to forty miles while pushing a 100-pound bag of cement in Rick's running and biking chairs. Dick and his son have since competed in and finished four Ironman competitions.

They have also biked and run across the United States, from Los Angeles to Boston, covering 3,735 miles in forty-five days, without a single day off. And after completing fifteen Boston marathons—the race where they were initially rejected back in 1981—they were honored on the marathon's 100th anniversary as the event's centennial heroes.

Dick still insists it's his son, not him, who is the athlete. "I don't know what it is, but when I get behind his chair, something happens. Rick is the driving force of the team. I loan him my body, but it's Rick's spirit that keeps us going."

Rick and Dick Hoyt have been competing for twenty years and say there's no end in sight. Winning the race is not all that important to them because they know that from the moment they take the starting line, every race is a victory.

CYNTHIA KERSEY

153. Never forget that the highest reward for your toil will not be what you will get for it, but what you will become by it.

JOHN RUSKIN

Real joy comes not from ease, riches, or from the praise of men, but from doing something worthwhile.

SIR WILFRED GRENFELL

Exert Effort

"When nothing seems to help, I go and look at the stonecutter hammering away at his rock perhaps a hundred times without as much as a crack showing in it. Yet on the hundred and first blow the rock will split in two, and I know it was not that blow that did it, but all that had gone before."

JACOB RIIS

154. You may have the loftiest goals, the highest ideals, the noblest dreams, but remember this: Nothing works unless you do.

NIDO QUBEIN

The only place where "success" comes before "work" is in the dictionary.

VIDAL SASSOON

155. Always remember that there is no elevator to success. You have to take the stairs.

DAVID STARR JORDAN

The reason people don't recognize Opportunity is because it wears overalls and looks a lot like Hard Work.

THOMAS EDISON

The formula for success is simple. It is found in ten little two-letter words:

"If it is to be, it is up to me."

ANONYMOUS

156. Don't waste time waiting for inspiration. The great composer does not set to work because he is inspired, but becomes inspired because he is working. Beethoven, Bach, and Mozart settled down day after day to the job at hand with as much regularity as an accountant settles down each day to his figures.

ERNEST NEWMAN

A professional is one who does his best work when he feels least like working.

FRANK LLOYD WRIGHT

157. When you follow your dream you should hope and work, but never hope more than you work.

H. JACKSON BROWN

Backbone beats wishbone every time.

WILL HENRY

158. Roll up your sleeves and plunge both hands into life up to the elbows.

JEAN ANOUILH

I always gave total effort, even when the odds seemed entirely against me.

ARNOLD PALMER

Did you know?

The Wright Brothers' initial twelve seconds of flight at Kitty Hawk, North Carolina, in their homemade airplane, was the result of thirteen years of research and testing.

Wilbur and Orville's father, Bishop Milton Wright, thought that flying should be "reserved for the angels and the birds," as God intended, and to even speak of flying was blasphemy and "nonsense."

He later changed his mind, and even consented to a ride in his sons' plane. Those on the ground could hear the elder Wright screaming from the air, "Higher, Orville, higher!"

The Power of Determination

No one knows what he can do until he tries.

PUBLILIUS SYRUS

A number of years ago in Elkhart, Kansas, a little boy had a job at his local school. He was assigned to start a fire in the potbellied stove in the classroom each morning.

One cold day, he cleaned out the stove and loaded it with firewood. Grabbing a can of kerosene, he doused the wood and lit the fire. An explosion then rocked the old building. It was later discovered that the kerosene can had accidentally been filled with gasoline. The fire severely burned the little boy to the point of death.

The doctor attending to the injured lad recommended amputating the young fellow's legs. The parents were devastated, but they did not lose their faith. They asked the doctor for a postponement of the amputation, and he consented. Each day they asked the doctor for a delay, praying that their son's legs would somehow heal and that he would become well again. For two months, the parents and the doctor debated on whether to amputate. They used this time to instill in the boy the belief that he would walk again someday.

They never amputated the boy's legs, but when the bandages were finally removed, it was discovered that his right leg was now almost three inches shorter than the left leg. Also, the toes on the left foot were almost completely burned off.

Yet the boy was fiercely determined. Though in excruciating pain, he forced himself to exercise daily until he could finally take a few painful steps. Slowly, ever so slowly, he began to recover. Finally, after years of struggle, he was able to throw away his crutches and to walk awkwardly on his own, and then to walk almost normally. Soon he was running…and run he did!

This determined young man kept running and running and running until those legs that came so close to being amputated carried him to Madison Square Gardens where he set a record for the fastest mile ever run.

His name? Glenn Cunningham. He was known thereafter as the "World's Fastest Human Being" and was named Athlete of the Century.

Cunningham may have had difficulty standing up on the outside when he first began his dream, but he was standing up from within all along.

GLENN VAN EKEREN

159. Accept the fact that your physical and intellectual development will be the result of effort, and effort means work.

CALVIN COOLIDGE

There are no shortcuts to any place worth going.

BEVERLY SILLS

160. You can have the results you say you want, or you can have all the reasons in the world why you can't have them. But you can't have both. Reasons or results. Choose.

SUSAN CARLSON

If you really want to do something, you'll find a way; if you don't, you'll find an excuse.

FRANK BANKS

What it Takes

To get profit without risk, experience without danger, or reward without work is as impossible as it is to live without being born.

A. P. GOUTHEY

Helping the deaf to communicate was Alexander Graham Bell's motivation for his life work, perhaps because his mother and his wife were both deaf. "If I can make a deaf-mute talk," Bell said, "I can make metal talk."

For five frustrating and impoverished years, he experimented with a variety of materials in an effort to make a metal disk that, vibrating in response to sound, could reproduce those sounds and send them over an electrified wire.

During a visit to Washington D.C., he called on Joseph Henry, a scientist who was a pioneer in electrical research. Graham presented his ideas to him and asked his advice—should he let someone else perfect the telephone or should he do it himself? Henry encouraged him to do it himself, to which Bell complained that he lacked the necessary knowledge of electricity. Henry's brief answer was: "Then get it."

And so, Bell studied electricity. A year later when he obtained a patent for the telephone, the Patent Office officials credited him with knowing more about electricity than all the other inventors combined.

GOD'S LITTLE DAILY DEVOTIONAL

A man with ambition can do more with a rusty screwdriver than a loafer can do with a shop full of tools.

GERMAN PROVERB

161. If you want your dreams to come true, don't spend too much time sleeping.

ANONYMOUS

Prove that you know the worth of time by employing it well.

LOUISA MAY ALCOTT

162. Seize the day!

HORACE

I never knew a man of greatness or eminence who lay in bed late in the morning.

JONATHON SWIFT

163. The future is yours to channel in the direction you want to go. You must continually ask yourself, "What will happen if…?" or better still, "How can I make that happen?"

LISA TAYLOR

Every time I burst into the house with some new dream or ambition, my father would be waiting in the living room to ask me one simple question: "How do you plan to do that?" And it wasn't a rhetorical question. I was expected to list every step I planned to take.

MICHAEL JOHNSON

164. Never forget that the will to win is not nearly as important as the will to prepare to win.

ANONYMOUS

I visualized where I wanted to be, what kind of player I wanted to become. I knew exactly where I wanted to go, and I focused on getting there.

MICHAEL JORDAN

165. Make your life a mission, not an intermission.

ARNOLD H. GLASGOW

Boys, there ain't no free lunch in this world, so don't go spending your whole life commiserating that you got a raw deal. You've got to say, "I think that if I keep working at this and want it bad enough I can have it." It's called perseverance.

LEE IOCOCCA

166. Get moving! Success comes to the person who does today what you were thinking about doing tomorrow.

ANONYMOUS

Things may come to those who wait, but only the things left by those who hustle.

ABRAHAM LINCOLN

The Sky is the Limit

The people who get on in this world are the people who get up and look for the circumstances they want. And if they can't find them, they make them.

GEORGE BERNARD SHAW

Eddie was third of eight children. His father's sudden death forced him to leave school and work in a glass factory to help support his mother and the younger children.

But Eddie was fascinated by cars. One afternoon he walked up to the head mechanic of an automobile plant in Columbus, Ohio, and stood silently before him. When the man finally looked at the boy, Eddie announced he was coming to work there the following morning.

"You are?" said the chief. "Who hired you?"

"Nobody yet," Eddie answered truthfully. "And if I'm not worth anything, then you can fire me…even though you didn't hire me."

The next morning Eddie had half the shop floor cleaned before the chief came to work. The chief was impressed with the lad, so Eddie was allowed to stay and work in the car plant.

Shortly afterwards, the chief saw him studying a booklet about carburetors on his lunch hour, and Eddie got transferred to the carburetor department.

Other promotions came quickly for the hardworking boy. Eddie became a branch manager, and then moved into sales.

To sell cars, he had to demonstrate them. And so Eddie Rickenbacker became an accomplished racing driver—and later a flying ace, and then President of Eastern Airlines.

SALES UPBEAT

167. Remember that success can look easy—and even undeserved—to those who were not around when it was being earned.

ARCHIE K. DAVID

I'm a great believer in luck, and I find that the harder I work, the more I have of it.

THOMAS JEFFERSON

168. Do not squander time.

BENJAMIN FRANKLIN

When I hear congratulations tendered to a man on his "luck" in achieving success—or when I am greeted in a similar fashion after a courtroom victory—I am inclined to recall that this type of "luck" usually visits me at 2:00 a.m. on a cold morning when, red-eyed and bone weary, I am poring over law books preparing a case. It never visits me when I'm at the movies, on the golf course, or when I'm reclining in an easy chair.

LOUIS NIZER

169. Understand that you will never "find" time for anything. If you want time you must make it.

CHARLES BUXTON

Time is a created thing. To say, "I don't have time" is like saying, "I don't want to."

LAO TZU

170. Once you have decided what you are trying to create, work out exactly what acts will be perfectly aligned to the creation of that reality. Nothing happens without action.

A. C. PING

When I was forty and looking at sixty, it seemed like a thousand miles away. Now I am sixty-two and it feels like a week and a half away from eighty. I must get on with the things I always talked about doing but put off.

HARRY BELAFONTE

A year from now you will wish you had started today.

KAREN LAMB

When I ask, “What can I do?” I’ve found the answer by rearranging the words: “Do what I can.”

TED MENTEN

171. Remember that the biggest gap in the world is between "I should" and "I did."

H. JACKSON BROWN

What one does is what counts and not what one has the intention of doing.

PABLO PICASSO

172. Ask yourself if what you are doing today is getting you closer to where you want to be tomorrow.

H. JACKSON BROWN

No matter how much time you've wasted in the past, you still have an entire tomorrow. Success depends upon using time wisely—by planning and setting priorities. Time is worth more than money, and by killing time, we are killing our own chances for success.

DENNIS WAITLEY

Classrooms Come in a Variety of Settings

Go to the ant. Consider her ways and be wise.

PROVERBS 6:6

Class was in session, and the teachers were all around me—ants. From my desk of worn and patchy lawn, I awaited the wisdom that would be taught to me in Nature's University—this place without chalkboards, textbooks, or walls.

Observation revealed that an ant can pull a dead grasshopper (the community's future food supply) across the dirt with a determination exceeding mathematical probability—in excess of fifty times its own weight!!

The struggle went on until it caught the attention of other ants.

The others then, without a leader to tell them what to do, hurried to help. They bumped into one another as they tried to grab hold of the gigantic bug, but no one stopped to fight about it. No one was arguing for a different or a better spot to pull from. No one seemed to be concerned about who was doing more or less work, or who would get the most credit. Their efforts were clearly focused beyond themselves and onto the whole of the good for all.

Watching them march toward their anthill, I pondered their astonishing strength and exceptional cooperation when another example flew by, its engine buzzing at full throttle—a bumble bee.

Scientists have made the conclusion that it is aerodynamically impossible for the bumble bee to fly. Its wings are too small and its body is too large. Yet the yellow, striped flying vessel continues to go "up, up and away," knowing nothing of the meaning of aerodynamics nor impossibility.

ROCHELLE PENNINGTON

"I hated every minute of the training, but I said, 'Don't quit. Suffer now and live the rest of your life as a champion.'"

MUHAMMAD ALI, Boxing Champion

Did you know?

A person has better odds of winning the lottery than of making a National Basketball Association team. Now add to the equation being only 5'3" tall, a full sixteen inches shorter than the average NBA player, like Tyrone Bogues. His life-long dream was to become a professional basketball player, but no one took Tyrone Bogues serious except Tyrone Bogues. His belief alone launched his dream and made him the smallest player in NBA history.

CYNTHIA KERSEY

173. Spend time wisely. It is more valuable than money. Money mistakes can be corrected, but time is gone forever.

DAVID B. NORRIS

If we would only give, just once, the same amount of reflection to what we want to get out of life that we give to the question of what we want to do with a two weeks' vacation, we would be startled at the aimless procession of our busy days.

DOROTHY CANFIELD FISHER

174. Understand that life is what you make it. Opportunities will always be there, but if you snooze, you will lose. And if you snore, you will lose more.

PHYLLIS GEORGE

None of the secrets of success will work unless you do.

VIC HARVILLE

A Home Run Effort

The best place to succeed is where you are with what you have.

CHARLES SCHWAB

If Pete Gray were here, he would tell you that self-motivation, determination, and action are the keys to personal success. And he should know. At six years old, Pete lost his arm in a freak farm accident. While trying to jump onto a slow-moving wagon, he missed, fell off, and caught his right arm in the wheel spokes. The arm was badly mangled. Doctors said there was no way to save it, so the arm was amputated just above the elbow.

The accident literally cut off the key to his dreams—or did it? Pete Gray was right-handed and desired more than anything to become a major league baseball player. Did he give up his dream? Not on your life!

Pete Gray learned to bat from his left side. He focused all his efforts on strengthening his left arm and mastering its control. His sharp eye and brilliant "magic" produced well-laid bunts, screaming line drives, and unbelievable distance.

As a semi-pro, his fielding acrobatics entertained the crowds. Pete Gray wore his glove on his fingertips. After catching the ball, he would quickly stick the glove under the stump of his right arm, grab the ball with his left arm, and throw. As amazing as it may seem, very little time was lost in this systematic approach.

While playing for the Memphis Chicks, Pete Gray began making a reputation for himself. In 1944 he batted .333, stole sixty-three bases, and was named the league's most valuable player. In two seasons of play, he struck out only fifteen times. His determination and baseball success made Pete Gray a household word. Even the U.S. government began filming his unusual yet effective style of play to show to wounded veterans. His story became an inspiration to many.

Finally, in 1945, Pete Gray's dream became a reality. Despite periodic personal doubts, discouragement from others, and, of course, his physical disability, Pete Gray signed a major league contract with the St. Louis Browns.

THE SPEAKER'S SOURCEBOOK

Grind it out!

"Rejection is the rough draft of a writer's success story."

NOREEN AYRES

Jane Austen, author of the bestselling book *Pride and Prejudice*, struggled for seventeen years while she searched for a publisher who was willing to print her book.

It took George Bernard Shaw, the world-famous author/playwright, nine years to earn his first twenty dollars as a writer.

Louis L'Amour, author of novels with over 300 million copies in print, received several hundred rejections before he made his first sale.

Dr. Seuss's first book was rejected by forty-three publishers.

Alex Haley's manuscript *Roots* was turned down by over two hundred publishers. Despite these rejections, Haley continued to press forward until his book was published and became a bestseller.

"I discovered that rejections are not altogether a bad thing. They teach a writer to rely on his own judgment and to say in his heart of hearts, 'To hell with you.'"

SAUL BELLOW

175. Realize that success is not going to come to you. You must go to it.

MARVA COLLINS

Persons who want milk should not seat themselves on a stool in the middle of a field in hopes that a cow will back up to them.

ELBERT HUBBARD

176. Don't look for something for nothing. It doesn't exist.

MATEL DAWSON, JR.

Success is one percent inspiration and ninety-nine percent perspiration.

THOMAS EDISON

You cannot cross the sea merely by standing on the shore and staring at the water.

RABINDRANATH TAGORE

177. Be ready to pay the price to make your dreams come true.

CARDINAL SUENENS

We can do whatever we wish to do provided our wish is strong enough. But the tremendous effort needed—one doesn't always want to make it—does one? But what else can be done? What is the alternative? What is it that we want most to do? That is the question we have to keep asking ourselves in the face of difficulties.

KATHERINE MANSFIELD

178. Study the lives of great men and famous women. You will find that the men and women who got to the top were those who did the jobs they had in hand with everything they had of energy, enthusiasm, and hard work.

HARRY S. TRUMAN

The man at the top of the mountain didn't just fall there.

ANONYMOUS

The Miracle Bridge

The Brooklyn Bridge which spans the river between Manhattan Island and Brooklyn is truly a miracle bridge. In 1883, a creative engineer named John Roebling was inspired by an idea for this spectacular bridge. However, bridge-building experts throughout the world told him to forget it; it could not be done.

Roebling convinced his son, Washington, who was a young, upcoming engineer, that the bridge could be built. The two of them developed the concepts of how it could be accomplished and how the obstacles could be overcome. With unharnessed excitement and inspiration, they hired their crew and began to build their dream bridge.

The project was only a few months under construction when a tragic accident on the site took the life of John Roebling and severely injured his son, Washington. Everyone felt that the project would have to be scrapped since the Roeblings were the only ones who knew how the bridge could be built. Even though Washington was unable to move or talk, his mind was as sharp as ever, and he still had a burning desire to complete the bridge. An idea hit him as he lay in his hospital bed, and he developed a code for communication. All he could move was one finger, so he touched the arm of his wife with that finger, tapping out a code to communicate to her what to tell the engineers who were building the bridge. For thirteen years, Washington tapped out his instructions with his finger until the spectacular Brooklyn Bridge was finally completed.

THE SPEAKERS SOURCEBOOK

179. Bear in mind that your own resolution to succeed will be more important than any other one thing.

ABRAHAM LINCOLN

Success has really one basic factor: "A sine qua non"—you must want it.

GEORGE EDWARD WOODBERRY

Did you know?

While training for the Olympics, Bruce Jenner arranged his entire apartment so that it would remind him every day of his goal. He put equipment from each of the ten sports he would be competing in during the decathlon in places where he couldn't help but encounter them during his non-training hours. Since the high hurdle was his weakest skill, he placed a hurdle right in the middle of his living room where he would have to step over it as many as thirty times a day. This "unusual décor"—a vaulting pole, a javelin, an iron shot, barbells—helped Bruce improve his form as he prepared for (and won!) the Olympic gold medal.

UNSTOPPABLE

180. Always remember that the golden opportunity you are seeking is in yourself. It is not in your environment. It is not in luck or chance or the help of others. It is in yourself alone.

ORISON SWETT MARDEN

The helping hand you need is at the end of your own arm.

SIDNEY J. PHIL

181. Follow your bliss.

JOSEPH CAMPBELL

Your work is to discover your work and then to give yourself to it with all of your heart.

BUDDHA

182. Don't allow your life to become one long postponement.

HENRY MILLER

"One of these days" becomes none of these days.

ANONYMOUS

183. Never forget that Procrastination is Opportunity's assassin.

VICTOR KIAM

Will you be satisfied with the fruit of your life's work? Will the efforts you are making now bring you satisfaction when the things of time are receding and eternity looms ahead?

RAYMOND COX

184. Be brave. Have faith. Go forward.

THOMAS EDISON

A longing fulfilled is sweet to the soul.

PROVERBS 13:19

Bibliography

They Did What!? by Bob Fenster; Andrews McMeel Publishing, Kansas City, MO; 2002

Forbes Greatest Business Stories of All Time by Daniel Gross; John Wiley & Sons, Inc., New York, NY; 1996

Forbes Great Success Stories by Alan Farnam; Wiley, New Jersey; 2000

Great Failures of the Extremely Successful by Steve Young; Tall Fellow Press, Los Angeles, CA; 2002.

Oops! by Paul Kirchner; General Publishing group, Santa Monica, CA; 1996

Panati's Extraordinary Endings of Practically Everything and Everybody by Charles Panati; Harper & Row, New York, NY; 1989

The Road to Success is Paved with Failure by Joey Green; Little Brown and Company, New York, NY; 2001

First Facts about American Heroes by David C. King; Blackbirch Press, New York, NY; 1996

When Life Gives You Lemons: Remarkable Stories of People Overcoming Adversity by Alex Tresniowski; McGraw-Hill, New York, NY; 2000

They All Laughed: From Light Bulbs to Lasers—The Fascinating Stories Behind the Great Inventions That Have Changed Our Lives by Ira Flatow; Harper, New York, NY; 1993

We Got Fired!...and It's the Best Thing That Ever Happened to Us by Harvey Mackay; Ballantine, New York, NY; 2004

The Incomplete Book of Failures by Stephen Pile; E. P. Dutton, New York, NY; 1979

They Went Broke?! by Roland Gary Jones; Gramercy Books, New York, NY; 2002

Fascinating Facts by David Louis; Crown Publishers, New York, NY; 1983

When They Were Kids by Carol Orsag Madigan and Ann Elwood; Random House, New York, NY; 1998

The World Almanac and Book of Facts; Scripps Howard, New York, NY; 1996

The Book of Strange Facts and Useless Information by Scott Morris; Doubleday, Garden City, New York; 1979

Some Days Nothing Goes Right by Michael Paggie; Barnes & Noble, New York, NY; 1993

Turn Hurts into Halos by Robert Schuller; Nelson, Nashville, TN; 1999

The Survivor Personality by Al Siebert; The Berkley Publishing Group, a division of Penguin Putnam, Inc., New York, NY; 1996

Hope Dies Last: Keeping the Faith in Difficult Times by Studs Terkel; The New Press, New York, NY; 2003

The Power of Failure by Charles C. Manz; Berrett-Koehler Publishers, Inc., San Francisco, CA; 2002

How They Achieved by Lucinda Watson; John Wiley & Sons, Inc., New York, NY; 2001

Unstoppable by Cynthia Kersey; Sourcebooks, Inc., Naperville, IL; 1998

Rich Dad's Success Stories by Robert T. Koyosaki; Warner Books, New York, NY; 2003

Extraordinary Comebacks by John A. Sarkett; Sourcebooks, Naperville, IL; 2007

Dare to Dream by Sandra McLeod Humphrey; Prometheus Books, Amherst, NY; 2005

Famous Failures by Joey Green; Lunatic Press, Los Angeles, CA; 2007

The True Joy of Positive Living by Norman Vincent Peale; William Morrow & Company; New York, NY; 1984

The Most Intriguing People of the Century; People Books, New York, NY; 1997

The 100 Most Influential Women of All Time by Deborah G. Felder; Citadel, New York, NY; 1996

How to Stop Worrying and Start Living by Dale Carnegie; Pocket Books, New York, NY; 1944

Most Remarkable Occurrences by John Train; HarperCollins, New York, NY; 1990

True Remarkable Occurrences by John Train; Clarkson N. Potter, Inc. Publisher, New York, NY; 1978

The Misfortune 500 by Bruce and Zullo Nash; Pocket Books, New York, NY; 1988

Late Bloomers by Brendan Gill; Artisan, New York, NY; 1996

The Books of Lists by David Wallechinsky, Irving Wallace, and Amy Wallace; Bantam, New York, NY; 1977

The Book of Lists 2 by Irvin Wallace, David Wallechinsky, Amy Wallace, and Sylvia Wallace; Morrow, New York, NY; 1980

Hoover's Handbook of American Business; Reference Press, Austin, Texas; 1995

Facts and Fallacies: A Book of Definitive Mistakes and Misguided Predictions by Chris Morgan and David Langford; Webb & Bower Limited, Devon, England; 1981

The Complete Directory to Prime Time Network TV Shows by Tim Brooks and Earle Marsh; Ballantine, New York, NY; 1992

The Film Encyclopedia by Ephraim Katz; Perigee, New York, NY; 1979

The TV Encyclopedia by David Inman; Perigee, New York, NY; 1991

How I Broke Into Hollywood by Pablo Fenjves & Rocky Lang; HarperCollins Publishers, New York, NY; 2006

Film Flubs by Bill Givens; Carol Publishing Group, New York, NY; 1990

Encyclopedia of Rock Stars by Dafydd Rees and Luke Crampton; DK, New York, NY; 1996

Encyclopedia of Sports in the United States by Kevin Osborn; Scholastic, New York, NY; 1997

The Hollywood Hall of Shame by Harry and Michael Medved; Putnam Publishing Group, New York, NY; 1984

Time Almanac Reference Edition; Compact, Washington D.C.; 1994

Rumor Has It by Bob Tamarkin; Prentice Hall General Reference, New York, NY; 1993

The Earth is Flat—and Other Great Mistakes by Laurence Pringle; William Morrow and Company, New York, NY; 1983

Complete and Utter Failure by Neil Steinberg; Doubleday, New York, NY; 1994

Foibles, Follies, and Foolish Deeds by Robert Cooper; Signet, New York, NY; 1993

Whatever Became of? (11th Edition) 100 Profiles of the Most Asked-About Movie, TV, and Media Personalities. Hundreds of Never-Before Published Facts, Dates, etc. on Celebrities by Richard Lamparski; Crown, New York, NY; 1989

Winning Every Day: The Game Plan for Success by Lou Holtz; Collins, New York, NY; 1999

The Best, Worst, and Most Unusual by Bruce Felton and Mark Fowler; Galahad Books, New York, NY; 1994

Flight Plan by Brian Tracy; Berrett-Koehler Publishers, Inc., San Francisco, CA; 2008

Copyright Acknowledgments

"A Herculean Effort" by Cynthia Kersey from *Unstoppable* (originally titled "Road Warriors of a Different Kind") used by permission of Sourcebooks, Inc., Naperville, IL. Copyright 1998.

"He Dared to Dream" by Sandra McLeod Humphrey (originally titled "Ben Carson") from the book *Dare to Dream* used by permission of Prometheus Books, Amherst, NY. Copyright 2005.

"H. J. Heinz" by Roland Gary Jones from *They Went Broke?!*, published by Gramercy Books. Copyright 1999, 2002. Used by permission.

"The Kid Stays in the Picture" by Fran Lostys and "Failing His Way to Success" by Janice Leary used by permission of *Readers Digest*.

Excerpts from *The Power of Failure* by Charles Manz ("From a Hotel Swimming Pool to the Olympics" and the NASA "Did You Know?" entry) used by permission of Berrett-Koehler Publishers, Inc., San Francisco, CA. Copyright 2002.

Public Domain inclusions: "As You Think" by James Allen, "Man Enough for the Job" by Ella Lyman Cabot, "Don't Quit" by Edgar Guest, and "The Magic Sword," Anonymous.

"A Fighting Spirit" used by permission of Endless Human Potential.

Excerpts from *The Sower's Seeds* series of books by Brian Cavanaugh used by permission of Paulist Press. (Available at bookstores or www.paulistpress.com or 1-800-218-1903.)

"Strong in Broken Places" by John Sarkett (originally titled "Max Cleland") from *Extraordinary Comebacks* used by permission of Sourcebooks, Inc., Naperville, IL. Copyright 2007.

Excerpts from *Bits and Pieces* magazine used by permission of Ragan Communications, Chicago, IL.

Excerpts from *Sales Upbeat* magazine used by permission of The Economics Press, Fairfield, NJ.

Excerpts from Mark Link used by permission of R.C.I., Allen, TX.

Excerpts by H. Jackson Brown, Jr., author of *The Complete Life's Little Instruction Book*, used by permission of Rutledge Hill Press, Nashville, TN. Copyright 1997.

"A Home Run Effort," "The Power of Perseverance," and "The Power of Determination" by Glenn Van Ekeren from *The Speaker's Sourcebook*. Copyright 1988. Used by permission of Penguin Putnam, New York, NY.

"Improvising Under Pressure" and "What it Takes" from *God's Little Daily Devotional*. Copyright 1997. Used by permission of Honor Books/Cook Communications Ministries, Colorado Spring, CO.